PRAISE FOR

JESUS UNTANGLED

"For more than a generation in Americanized Christianity, Jesus has become so entangled in the political realm that he has become more of a political pawn to be owned by a side, than a leader to follow into uncharted territory. His message, once so counter-cultural, has been stifled, suffocated, and reduced to a tangled pile of knots on the floor of the American political scene. I can think of no better place for a Christian to begin sorting those out, and reclaiming a message that is still other-worldly after all these years, than with *Jesus Untangled.*"

– BENJAMIN L. COREY, AUTHOR OF *UNDILUTED: REDISCOVERING THE RADICAL MESSAGE OF JESUS*

"This important book clears away the sticky webs that entangle the people of God. It demands the people of Jesus to look like Jesus, and not the world. It demands attention. Disagree with it. Debate it. Deal with it, or just do it...but dismiss it at your own peril."

– NEIL COLE, AUTHOR AND FOUNDER OF CHURCH MULTIPLICATION ASSOCIATES

"In *Jesus Untangled,* Keith Giles has put into words the cries and moans my heart has been making for years. This book could have been called *Jesus Unstrangled* because Keith is pumping oxygen back into our relationship with Christ and helping release the chokehold of American Churchianity. If your blood runs red, white, and blue while your faith sits meek and mild then I dare you to read this book!"

– KENT C. WILLIAMSON, EMMY-NOMINATED DIRECTOR OF *BY WAR & BY GOD*

"I joined the US Navy because I thought Jesus wanted me to kill America's enemies. My faith in God was tangled with my faith in America. Untangling my faith has been a hard journey that's taken many years. *Jesus Untangled* introduces the main ideas that led me on my journey."

– MIKE IZBICKI, FORMER U.S. NAVAL OFFICER AND CONSCIENTIOUS OBJECTOR

"Through passionate stories, cultural commentary, and biblical insight, Keith Giles presents a good case for separating politics from following Jesus. We shouldn't want a 'Christian' nation, because no worldly nation can ever follow the values and guidelines of Jesus. The rule and reign of God doesn't come through laws, regulations, and votes, but through God's people living like Jesus among the people he brings around us. Do you want to change the world? Follow Jesus wherever he leads."

– JEREMY MYERS, AUTHOR AND BIBLE TEACHER AT REDEEMINGGOD.COM

"Our allegiance to God has been compromised by allegiance to earthly politics, and many of us don't even realize it. But we can only serve one master. In *Jesus Untangled*, Keith Giles provides a desperately needed wake-up call to the church in America, exposing the dangers of nationalism, and showing how Jesus offered a better way—the way of self-sacrificial love. This book should be in the hands of every American Christian."

– CHUCK MCKNIGHT, BLOGGER AT HIPPIEHERETIC.COM

"If there is an area that begs, yes screams, for untangling, it is the subtle or overt fusion (and resulting confusion) of God-and-Country. Years ago Jerry Falwell's church had a marquis that proclaimed—"Get 'em saved; get 'em registered." During WWI, preachers expressed sentiments like, "every dollar and every service given to Uncle Sam for his army is a gift to missions." James Dobson advised a mother concerned about her child being bullied, "I believe you should teach your child to defend himself/herself when attacked. Later, they can be taught to turn the other cheek." *Jesus Untangled* touches some of the most sensitive nerves in the religious world. You may struggle deeply with some of the details he presents, but Keith Giles does a superb job of uncovering the lie that wraps the flag or national symbol of any country around Jesus. Our allegiance is only to the Lamb of God."

– JON ZENS, AUTHOR OF *58-0: HOW CHRIST LEADS THROUGH THE ONE ANOTHERS*

"One of the trials Jesus faced in the desert was Satan's enticing offer of absolute political power. Christ's triumph over this temptation prepared him for his ministry to a people who were only looking for a political Messiah, who would one day try to make him king by force. Jesus didn't come to usurp political authority; he came to subvert it.

And for the first few hundred years, the church followed in his footsteps. Rather than being unequally yoked with the world, seduced by its political power, the first Christians lived as ambassadors of another Kingdom; they understood their one and only allegiance was to the Lamb, and their only true citizenship was in heaven.

But after years of persecution, Rome finally offered the church relief, along with influence. So, we laid to rest the real Christ, in his burial shroud, and resurrected a new Christ, wrapped in a national flag. And over time, we learned to view the Bible through the lens of our own political leanings and turn Scripture into a prooftext for political ambitions and agendas.

In his new book, *Jesus Untangled*, Keith Giles reveals an unentangled Christianity that is much more than a mere separation of church and state. He demolishes the recurring fantasy of a world transformed through Christian laws and policies, and reawakens us to the truly transformative power of the Gospel. Using compelling examples of Christians throughout history, along with a sound interpretation of Scripture, Keith skillfully argues for today's church to finally lay down the sword of politics, and once again take up the cross of Christ."

– RICHARD JACOBSON, AUTHOR OF *UNCHURCHING: CHRISTIANITY WITHOUT CHURCHIANITY* AND CO-HOST OF *THE UNCHURCHING PODCAST*

"Simply stated, every Kingdom-minded believer will benefit from reading *Jesus Untangled.* This is especially true in the hyper-sensitized, increasingly polarized and divisive society that we live in today. In a day when everyone is drawing lines and choosing sides, Keith asks us to 'Take a step back from everything you've ever been told, or seen modelled by other Christians, and try to see things from a different perspective than you might be used to.' If you are willing to take an open-minded journey with Keith on the topic of Christianity and politics, you will find things that you heartily agree with, things that intrigue or challenge you, and quite possibly things that evoke a resounding, 'No, No, NO!' But if you are brave enough to persevere, you will find yourself reevaluating, reassessing, and possibly repenting of attitudes and beliefs you have held about what it means to follow Jesus without entanglement."

– DAN NOTTI, BIBLE TEACHER AND CONFERENCE SPEAKER

OTHER BOOKS BY THE AUTHOR

- *The Top 10 Things Every Christian Should Know (But Probably Doesn't)*
- *Nobody Follows Jesus (So Why Should You?)*
- *The Gospel: For Here or to Go?*
- *[Subversive Interviews] Volume 1*
- *This Is My Body: Ekklesia as God Intended*
- *War Is Not Christian*
- *How to Start a Ministry to the Poor in Your Own Community*
- *The Power of Weakness*

Available online at: www.KeithGiles.com

JESUS UNTANGLED

CRUCIFYING OUR POLITICS TO PLEDGE ALLEGIANCE TO THE LAMB

KEITH GILES

First Edition

Cover design and layout by Rafael Polendo (polendo.net)

ISBN 978-1-938480-21-8

This volume is printed on acid free paper and meets ANSI Z39.48 standards.

Printed in the United States of America

Published by Quoir
Orange, California

www.quoir.com

DEDICATION

To my magnificent wife, Wendy. You are my inspiration.

ACKNOWLEDGEMENTS

Mike Yang, Ross Rohde, Chuck McKnight, Rafael Polendo, Herb Montgomery, Richard Jacobson, and everyone at the Mission House Church.

TABLE OF CONTENTS

Foreword by Greg Boyd 13

Introduction 23

1 The Problem: How Nationalism Hinders the Gospel 29

2 A Matter of Perspective 37

3 The Way We Were: The Church Before Entanglement 53

4 How We First Became Confused About Who We Really Are 61

5 The Weakness of Politics as an Agent of Change 75

6 The Supremacy of Christ and the Gospel 93

7 The Conspiracy of Entanglement 107

8 How American Empire Works 121

9 Why Your Vote Doesn't Count 129

10 The Power of Fear 133

11 Our National Identity Crisis 141

12 One Holy Nation 153

13 Tribalism and Violence 159

14 America: An Un-Christian Empire 167

15 Just War? 177

16 Living Untangled 187

Appendix: Revolving Door Politics 193

Endnotes 197

FOREWORD

Now that the 2016 Presidential Election in America is over, I'm sure you would agree with me that this was, hands-down, the craziest, nastiest, crudest, often funniest, most shocking and scandalous reality TV show you've ever watched! I mean, did any of you ever dream that American parents would have to make sure their children were not within hearing distance before they felt it was safe to turn on the evening news and find out what happened that day in the race for president?

Few would dispute that this has been a dark moment in the history of American politics. With both candidates in this election season up to their necks in scandals, and each setting historic records in the unfavorable department, many Christians on both the left and the right found very little in either candidate to enthusiastically endorse.

Consequently, for the first time in almost four decades, the church in my part of the country has remained relatively quiet throughout this election cycle. I, for one, want to scream: "Hallelujah! Praise be to Jesus!"

What is even better is this: Instead of trying to get their congregations to rally around particular candidates and positions as many pastors have done in past election seasons, a surprisingly large number of pastors I know have used the pulpit to talk about King Jesus and his Kingdom, even highlighting the radical ways this King and Kingdom contrasts with the kings and kingdoms of the world.

As disgusted as I am over the deplorable nature of this year's presidential contest, the fact that it has had this fortunate side effect makes me want to tap into my Pentecostal roots and start jumping pews and running aisles!

Having said this, isn't it bothersome that many Christians waited for an election season to put an emphasis on Jesus and his Kingdom? Do you, like me, find it a bit troubling that talking about King Jesus instead of political candidates from American pulpits had to come about as a side effect of a particularly dismal presidential race? I mean, where in the New Testament are we taught to rally around anyone other than King Jesus? Where do we find any hint of a suggestion in the New Testament that part of our job as followers of Jesus is to weigh in on the political disputes of the country we happen to live in?

We certainly don't find such a hint in the ministry of Jesus, whose example we're repeatedly commanded to follow.

Jesus lived in a time and place in which political hot topics were on everyone's mind. Among other things, first century Palestinian Jews were sharply divided over the "right" way to respond to the unjust and often abusive power that Rome exercised over them. Because most religious leaders of his day saw Jesus as a threat, they tried to undermine his popularity by getting him to weigh in on some of these topics. (Divisive ideological polarization in politics is clearly nothing new). However, in every instance, Jesus refused to take the bait. Instead of playing the political game of these leaders, Jesus wisely replaced each of their questions with a question that was more pertinent to the kingdom of God—the Kingdom which Jesus came to establish.

For example, Jesus was asked to weigh in on the hot topic of whether or not Jews should pay the taxes that Romans demanded of them—the very taxes that supported the Roman military that oppressed them. Instead of answering this question, however, Jesus showed the crowd a coin and asked them whose image was on it.

Of course, the coin bore the image of Caesar, which the Jews considered to be an idolatrous violation of the second of the Ten Commandments (Exodus 20:4). Jesus then said: "So give back to Caesar what is Caesar's, but give to God what is God's " (Matthew 22:21).

Do you see how Jesus ingeniously replaced the leaders' political question with his own Kingdom question? Holding up the idolatrous coin, Jesus was in essence saying:

"Are we Jews really going to bicker with each other about how much of this idolatrous metal we should cling to? Since it all bears Caesar's image, give all back to him! The only important question we ought to be wrestling with is whether or not we are giving back to God all that bears his image—namely, our whole self."

Jesus clearly hadn't come to give people the "right" answer to their many questions surrounding secular politics. His mission didn't include providing people with a new-and-improved version of the kingdoms of this world, even though he certainly had the opportunity to do so! People wanted to enthrone him as their worldly king, but Jesus ran away from them when they tried (John 6:15). And although the devil offered him all the "authority" and "splendor" of "all the kingdoms of the world," Jesus wisely declined the offer (Luke 4:5-7).

Just think for a moment of all the practical good he could have done had he accepted the devil's offer of supreme political power! He could have instantly alleviated all the unjust suffering his people were enduring under Rome, which is precisely what the Jewish people expected the Messiah to do—and precisely why they wanted to make him king. In fact, Jesus could have instantly transformed every government into the most just and most benevolent form of government the world has ever seen or imagined!

Yet, pragmatic advantages notwithstanding, Jesus saw the possibility of embracing all this political power as a temptation of the devil. And this forces this all-important question: If Jesus viewed the desire to acquire political power to be a temptation of the devil, why do so many American Christians fight to acquire as much of this political power as they can?

So too, if Jesus refused to weigh in on divisive political issues, choosing instead to keep his attention singularly focused on advancing the kingdom of the Father who sent him, why do so many American Christians chose to divert their attention away from the kingdom of God as they spend time and energy fighting to defend the "right" side of political disputes?

The answer that is always given in response to questions like this is that there are practical, good things that can be accomplished by gaining political power. Perhaps so, but we just saw that pragmatic considerations didn't alter Jesus' view that the quest for political power was a temptation from Satan. Moreover, this pragmatic answer fails to consider all the practical, good things that the church fails to do, for the glory of our King, because so many Christians are preoccupied trying to tell government what good things it should do.

As Keith Giles argues in this clear, insightful, and very readable book, the sad truth is that this quest for political power is the result of the American church allowing Herself to be co-opted by political power. In fact, the even sadder truth is that this has been more or less true of the church as a whole since the fourth century when the church first caved in to the very same temptation that Jesus resisted.

For reasons that Keith discloses in this book, a Roman emperor named Constantine believed (mistakenly) that Jesus had helped him win an important battle. As a result, Constantine decided to invest the church with wealth and political power. Tragically, instead of following the example of Jesus by interpreting this offer as a temptation of Satan, church leaders like Eusebius and Augustine interpreted this offer as a blessing of God!

As Keith masterfully illustrates, it was at this time that the Church began to forget that the kingdom of God, which we are called and empowered to advance, always reflects the loving, self-sacrificial, enemy-embracing character of Jesus, never the harsh, self-serving, enemy-hating character that typifies the kingdoms of the world. We forgot that Christians are called to follow the way of the cross, not the way of political power in which people fight to impose their (assumed) morally and intellectually superior convictions on others. We forgot that we are called and empowered to address social issues and further the transformation of the world, not by trusting in the power of laws and policies—let alone bullets and bombs—but by trusting in the power of the cross, which is the very power of God (1 Corinthians 1:18, 24).

We are to impact society not by voicing our opinions about what government should do, but by demonstrating what we as a church are willing to do as we sacrifice our time, money, talent and privileges to help all who are hungry, homeless, oppressed, lost, judged and suffering from discrimination.

Jesus Untangled is a clarion call for Christians to wake up to the many ways we have compromised our distinct calling as citizens of the kingdom of God by becoming entangled with the affairs of the kingdom of the world. It is a prophetic call for us to remember, and to never again forget, that we are soldiers of God's kingdom, stationed in enemy occupied territory—though our enemy is never "flesh and blood," but the "spiritual forces of evil in the heavenly realms" (Ephesians 6:12).

As Paul instructs us, we must therefore never allow ourselves to get "entangled in civilian affairs," but must instead remain singularly focused on our efforts "to please [our] commanding officer," Jesus Christ (2 Timothy 2:4).

Jesus Untangled is a heart-felt, urgent plea for Christians to embrace the truth that they are ambassadors who are not called to invest their energy engaging in the political fights of this land in which we are stationed. We are rather called to represent the radically different and altogether beautiful King and Kingdom of Heaven (2 Corinthians 5:19-20).

I would like to end with a word of warning, followed by a word of encouragement. If you are a typical American Christian who has not previously heard the message of how the Kingdom of God radically contrasts with the kingdoms of the world, I feel compelled to tell you up front that this book will likely call into question foundational assumptions about America, about the Gospel, and about a host of other things that you may have cherished since childhood. Indeed, if you more or less share the typical American Christian view of God and country, this book will challenge you to undergo a complete paradigm shift.

Having undergone this paradigm shift myself, I know full well how unsettling it can be. You may at times find yourself getting angry, anxious, and/or depressed. You may even be tempted to simply throw the book aside. If you find yourself in this place, I implore you to resist this temptation and to keep reading! If and when you find yourself being disturbed by an argument or position Keith defends, I encourage you to focus on one all-important question: Does Keith's perspective accurately reflect the teachings and example of Jesus as well as the teaching of the whole New Testament? Along these lines, you might find it helpful to read this book with a Bible next to you so you can check out for yourself the passages Keith cites and compare Scripture with Scripture on your own.

If you patiently work through whatever discomfort you may experience while reading this book, and if you honestly evaluate Keith's arguments in light of Scripture, I strongly suspect you will find what an increasing number of people around the globe are finding these days. At some point, I suspect you will find yourself waking up to a King and a Kingdom that is far more radical, far more beautiful, and far more powerful in transforming you and your surrounding culture than you had ever heard or imagined.

And, as is true of Keith, myself, and a growing multitude of others, I suspect you will soon find your heart grieves when you see, with increasing degrees of poignant clarity, the ways in which the radical and beautiful and powerfully transforming nature of this King and this Kingdom has become so banal, unattractive, and powerless by having become entangled with the kings and kingdoms of this world.

– Gregory A. Boyd

Senior Pastor, Woodland Hills Church, Maplewood, MN; author of *The Myth of a Christian Nation* (Zondervan, 2006) and numerous other books.

"CHRISTIANITY IS SO ENTANGLED WITH THE WORLD THAT MILLIONS NEVER GUESS HOW RADICALLY THEY HAVE MISSED THE NEW TESTAMENT PATTERN. COMPROMISE IS EVERYWHERE."

—A.W.TOZER

INTRODUCTION

"Nationalism does nothing but teach you to hate people you never met and to take pride in accomplishments you have no part in."

– DOUG STANHOPE

Do you know what you get when you mix religion and politics? *You get politics.*

That's an old joke, but it's more true than most Christians want to admit—especially Christians in America. At least, that has been my observation over the last few decades.

A friend of mine once suggested that, today, many Christians are more American than Christian. I am beginning to think that he is right.

Many Christians are more likely to be moved to tears over the sound of the national anthem being played, or of someone quoting Ronald Reagan, than they are when someone reads the words of Jesus out loud. Many are enraged at the mere suggestion of someone disrespecting their flag, but they hardly bat an eye when someone contradicts the teachings of Jesus.

In the words of Paul, the Apostle, "My friends, this ought not to be."

It's this very entanglement that disturbs me most. When I see people who claim to love and follow Jesus placing more emphasis on the Constitution than the Sermon on the Mount, or living their daily lives according to their rights as American citizens rather than as surrendered servants of Christ, it greatly concerns me.

On a daily basis I interact with Christians who are constantly appealing to the Constitution, or one of the many amendments, as a basis for their behavior. Whenever I attempt to lovingly redirect these people to the person and character of Jesus as an example of how they should be viewing the world, I am consistently shouted down and accused of not being a real American, or of being a "liberal"—even though my appeal comes from the Gospel and isn't about politics at all.

SO, I HAVE BEEN AWARE OF THE FACT THAT MANY CHRISTIANS TODAY ARE WRESTLING WITH THE DIFFERENCES BETWEEN FOLLOWING JESUS AND BEING A GOOD CITIZEN.

So, I have been aware of the fact that many Christians today are wrestling with the differences between following Jesus and being a good citizen.

So, I wrote a blog post about it. That turned into a series of posts, and before I knew it I had written over a dozen articles about untangling Jesus from politics.

Those posts formed the bedrock of the book you're holding now.

Out of that series of articles, I had some very insightful and productive conversations with Christians about what it really means to follow Jesus, and about what we should do whenever we encounter tension between following Jesus and being an American citizen.

A lot of what I'm going to write about in this book will appeal to the example of the early Christian church. I do believe that there is a very rich vein of wisdom to be mined in the writings of the early church fathers on this topic—partly because they were so close in space and time to the Lord Jesus and His apostles, but also because they were living in a culture very similar to our own (with a few notable exceptions, of course).

Those early Christians did not vote. They were not members of a democracy, as we are here in America. They were not protected by any laws—at least not prior to the reign of Constantine and his apparent conversion in the 4th century.

They were also, prior to Constantine, not living in a pro-Christian culture. In fact, they were living in a culture that violently opposed them and their way of life, and often turned against them.

Perhaps that is where we can find some common ground with Christians like Tertullian, Ignatius and Origen? We, like those early Christian teachers, know what it's like to have a set of values and ideals that the rest of the world just doesn't seem to embrace.

As we look closer, I believe we'll find that we share even more similarities with them...but more about that later.

What I hope to do in this book is to convince you that being an American and following Jesus are not the same thing.

I also hope to demonstrate to you that any attempt to change the world through political power and influence is not only misguided, but it may even be anti-Christian and in direct opposition to the Gospel itself—as hard as that might be for you to accept right now.

For the time being, I would ask you to give me the benefit of the doubt. Take a few moments to consider the ideas and the Scriptures that I'm about to show you. Take a step back from everything you've ever been told, or seen modeled by other Christians, and try to see things from a different perspective than you might be used to.

When we're all done, I may not have changed your mind, but at least you will have taken the very brave steps to question your own beliefs and challenge your most dearly-held assumptions about faith and politics.

I don't know about you, but I think it's always a good idea to place our convictions on the anvil once in a while and hammer them out a little. Not just so we can watch the sparks fly, but so that we will know when we are done if our assumptions and beliefs can withstand the test.

Are you up for the challenge? I hope so.

To get us started, let me kick things off by asking you to consider something you might never have thought about before. Suppose someone in another country, let's say Communist China as an example, hears the Gospel and responds. They fully repent of their old life and they completely surrender their hearts and minds to the Lordship of Jesus Christ; taking up their cross to follow Him daily and living joyously for Him alone.

Now, does that person also become a capitalist or a Republican at the same time?

Hopefully your answer is "No, of course not." Although there have been times when people have said that this person would be better off if they did become a capitalist or a Republican, that is beside the point. The fact is that someone who hears the Gospel of Jesus and who sincerely responds to His call does not automatically become a conservative American with a particular set of political values.

That means that it is not only possible to follow Jesus with a sincere heart without being a conservative American citizen, it's being done all over the world this very minute.

Consider, also, that most of those who follow Christ in this world are not living in America. That means that the majority of our brothers and sisters in the Body of Christ are from other nations with very different ideologies and from radically divergent political streams of thought.

Consider also that following Jesus does not entail the acceptance of any set of man-made political values. The teachings of Jesus are for us as individuals and they contain challenges that touch our hearts and speak to our personal attitudes and behaviors. His commands are about how we love one another, and how we treat those around us. His Gospel is about drawing nearer to God and learning to be more like Him in every way.

We would find it very strange indeed if, in our little example, we went on to say that this Christian in communist China suddenly became more entangled in the politics of the Communist Party. We would probably be very disturbed to meet a Christian brother or sister who was passionately devoted to North Korea and fiercely prideful about their nationalism.

WE HAVE BEEN SO INUNDATED WITH THE IDEAS OF GOD AND COUNTRY THAT WE CAN BARELY IMAGINE ONE WITHOUT THE OTHER.

At least, I would hope so.

Yet, some of us see nothing wrong with mixing our Christian faith with our American nationalism. In fact, some not only see that as "normal," they can hardly imagine what it would be like to follow Jesus without embracing the flag, revering the Constitution, and weeping as the band plays the Star-Spangled Banner.

But is that normal Christianity? Or are we simply conditioned by our society or our religious leaders to mix our faith with our national pride?

For many Christians, this is a very large blind spot. We have been so inundated with the ideas of God and country that we can barely imagine one without the other.

Nevertheless, we must admit that it is possible to follow Jesus apart from politics—even if we aren't sure exactly how to do that, or what it might look like. My hope, in this book, is to show you that it is not only possible, but that it is also very, very necessary to do so.

In this book, I also want to ask a few important questions. For example: How did this entanglement happen? Why is it so hard for us to disengage Christianity and nationalism?

That is what *Jesus Untangled* intends to explore. The answers we uncover may shock you, and perhaps even make you a little angry. However, when we're all done, this book might also fill you with hope and offer you a brand new perspective about how to follow Jesus—and only Jesus—without being polluted by outside influences like nationalism or politics.

At least, that is my sincere hope and prayer.

Are you ready? If so, let's begin.

CHAPTER 1

THE PROBLEM: HOW NATIONALISM HINDERS THE GOSPEL

"The only right a Christian has is the right to give up his rights."

– OSWALD CHAMBERS

Philip Yancey tells the story of something that happened to a friend of his in World War II during the Battle of the Bulge.[1] His friend was part of a special unit that was sent out each morning to kill wounded German soldiers who were left on the battlefield from the night before.

One morning his unit came across a German soldier who was sitting on the ground under a tree. He wasn't wounded. He was just too exhausted to move. Phil's friend raised his rifle and took aim, but the man said, in perfect English, "Please, give me just a moment to pray." Lowering his rifle Phil's friend said, "Are you a Christian?" and when the German soldier said "Yes, I am," his friend responded, "I am, too!"

Then the two of them sat together under the tree and Phil's friend pulled a Bible out of his jacket. They read a few Scriptures together and prayed for one another and for their families back home. After saying, "Amen," Phil's friend stood up, looked at his German brother in Christ and said, "I guess we'll meet again in Heaven one day," and then he shot the man in the head.

That horrific story illustrates the evils of nationalism better than anything else I could imagine. Here, we can see how devotion and allegiance to our nation can warp our theology and cause us to justify acts of violence and brutality that Jesus would never condone.

Nationalism denies the transcendent nature of God's Kingdom. It ignores the fact that there is one universal Body of Christ that includes those from every tongue, tribe, and nation. It twists us into tools of the State and drowns out the voice of Jesus that seeks to remind us that everyone we meet is our neighbor, made in the image of God, and is therefore worthy of love, grace, and mercy.

If we allow ourselves to become allured by nationalism, we are forgetting that God loves every person within every nation, not just the nation into which we were born. So, while we may believe that God loves our country, we must also remember that He also loves China, Mexico, Iran, and every single other nation on earth exactly the same. He is no respecter of persons. He even loves the just and the unjust equally.

For anyone who hopes to follow Jesus, there is no room to be a Christian and a nationalist at the same time. Not only does our nationalism divide our loyalties, but it actually dilutes our devotion to the teachings of Jesus and elevates the State and the interests of our nation above the kingdom of Christ.

As Paul put it, "No soldier in active service entangles himself in the affairs of everyday life, so that he may please the one who enlisted him as a soldier" (2 Timothy 2:4).

We are not called to participate in the affairs of this world. In fact, we are highly discouraged to do so in the New Testament

Scriptures. Jesus warns us to count the cost of becoming one of His disciples. Paul reminds us that we are ambassadors of Christ and of His Kingdom.

To further develop Paul's metaphor, every single person who is following Jesus has enlisted in the army of God. This army exists to defend the Gospel of the Kingdom and to engage in spiritual warfare against principalities and powers of the Enemy. Our aim is to overthrow the powers of darkness and to transform people from within by the power of the Holy Spirit.

Our victory is assured. Our General is unbeatable. Our weapons are powerful beyond measure. Nothing can stop us.

But, according to the Apostle Paul, there is something that can slow us down. He calls it "entanglement with the affairs of this life." Much like any soldier, we have to be on our guard against distractions. We cannot become too immersed in the nation we are assigned to liberate. We cannot allow ourselves to lay down our weapons in the pursuit of "civilian affairs," or we risk losing ground while endangering our fellow soldiers.

NO, THERE'S NOTHING WRONG WITH WANTING TO MAKE THE WORLD A BETTER PLACE. THE PROBLEM IS IN SEEKING TO DO SO WITHOUT JESUS—OR, WORSE, TO MIX CHRISTIANITY WITH POLITICS, AS IF ONE HAD NEED OF THE OTHER.

Politics is an integral part of the world system. Therefore, I believe it is one of the entanglements we must resolve to avoid. Honestly, I believe that political entanglement is one of the most dangerous kinds of entanglement we face in this battle, simply because those who become entangled in it do so out of a sincere desire to make a positive difference in the world.

Of course, every Christian hopes to make an impact on the world around them. This is part of why we are so eager to serve our Lord Jesus—because He has the best possible plan for changing the world from within, without oppression or violence.

No, there's nothing wrong with wanting to make the world a better place. The problem is in seeking to do so without Jesus—or, worse, to mix Christianity with politics, as if one had need of the other.

Politics is not about Jesus. Simply put, it's about power and influence. Nowadays, it is increasingly also about money, fame, manipulation, and compromise. Because of this, the follower of Jesus has no business becoming entangled in such a worldly, corrupt system.

Even if the Christian sincerely believes that they can make a difference through politics, the fact remains that the amount of good that might be accomplished in this way is often at the expense of one or more of their own Christian values. With politics, compromises must take place. Voters are often forced to choose between the lesser of two evils, which still amounts to choosing some option—or some politician—that is evil.

As C.H. Spurgeon once said, "Of two evils, choose neither."

Christians have only one choice, and that is Christ.

What's more, politics involves spending millions—sometimes billions—of dollars on campaign expenses. Just imagine if that same amount of money had been invested in the sharing of the Gospel, or in actually solving some of the problems facing actual citizens in our nation! How much better off would our world be if we abandoned the political process and simply shared our funds and invested our time directly with the people around us who are in need?

"But no political party would ever spend their money on the Gospel, or in helping advance the Kingdom, or in caring for the poor," you might say. To which I would reply, "Then why would any Christian entangle themselves with such a gigantic waste of money and empty use of time?"

We can rest assured that the nations will continue to seek political solutions to the problems of this world, as they have done for thousands of years. However, do Christians really need to become entangled in that endless, fruitless process?

We have better things to do. We are soldiers of the King. Our army is advancing daily. New recruits arrive ready for the battle even as we speak. Our Lord has spoken. We must engage the enemy. Entanglements only serve the interests of our foes.

One day, this battle will be over. Our Lord will descend from Heaven with a shout. And on that day, he will look over His troops. When He comes to you, will He see one who has lived as a stranger and an alien, untangled from civilian affairs? Or, will He see a soldier who tried to mix Christianity with politics and ended up with politics?

As Paul reminds us, "We are therefore Christ's ambassadors, as though God were making his appeal through us." (2 Corinthians 5:20)

As followers of Jesus, we are His representatives—specifically, his ambassadors—to the world around us. This speaks to the reality of Christ's Kingdom being separate from the kingdoms of this world, and of the need to bridge the gap between the two. That's our job.

As ambassadors, we are called to live out the customs and the values of Christ's Kingdom in this strange and alien land so that those who are natives here can see for themselves what life is like in the Kingdom of God.

What should people see when they look at us? They should see how we love one another. They should see how we love our neighbors. They should see how we love even our enemies.

They should see how we—in obedience to our King—handle conflict: by loving, forgiving, blessing, and serving those who come against us. They should see how we value the outcasts, love the poor, and how we care for those people that everyone else wants to ignore or marginalize.

When people look at us, they should see us acting as peacemakers when everyone else is crying out for war and bloodshed. They should see us living lives that are radically different from everyone who is not of our Father's Kingdom.

Here's what they should *not* see: They should never see us pledging allegiance to another nation. No ambassador would ever pledge allegiance to the nation to which he/she is sent. To do so would be considered treason. They should never see us living according to the customs of the land. Violence and a lust for power have no place in our King's heart, and it has no place in His Kingdom.

NO AMBASSADOR WOULD EVER PLEDGE ALLEGIANCE TO THE NATION TO WHICH HE/SHE IS SENT. TO DO SO WOULD BE CONSIDERED TREASON.

Certainly there is a time for being "all things to all people" so that some might come to know our King. However, we must always be careful to remember the values and customs of His Kingdom. Why? So that our lives may reflect the radical differences between these two opposing kingdoms.

Our job as ambassadors is to represent our King, and to provide a constant example of the contrast between those who live in His Kingdom and those who do not.

If anyone ever looks at our lives and becomes confused about that essential difference, then we have failed in our mission.

Some may suggest that it's possible to love two nations at once. For example, can't someone love both France and America? What would be the problem in that? Well, on the surface, nothing is wrong with that. At least until we discover that the leaders of one nation have declared war against the other. Now what? We cannot continue to maintain loyalty to both nations in that case. Now we need to make a choice. Are we going to stand with one nation, or with the other?

Make no mistake. The kingdoms of the world (which includes America) are man-made, self-serving political empires. They are not seeking to do God's will. They are at war with Christ and His Kingdom. They oppose Jesus and His commands. They mock His agenda. They ignore the values of His Kingdom (love, mercy, justice, grace, compassion, service, etc.) and embrace the values of this world (war, violence, torture, exploitation, greed, lust, etc).

The Kingdom of God and the American empire are not congruent. They are not complimentary. They are opposing forces with radically different goals, values and ideals.

Just ask yourself: Does my nation officially devote itself to the specific person of Jesus? Does my nation acknowledge Jesus alone as Lord and King? Does my nation base any of its laws or policies on the Sermon on the Mount? If you answered "No" to any (or all) of those questions, your nation is not Christian and it stands against the Kingdom of our Lord.

> "You adulterous people, don't you know that friendship with the world means enmity against God? Therefore, anyone who chooses to be a friend of the world becomes an enemy of God" (James 4:4).

Certainly, we could decide to remain neutral and just wait to see which nation wins the war. However, in our case, we already know which nation is going to win—the Kingdom of God. So, we have to choose: do we pledge allegiance to an earthly nation, or to the Kingdom of God?

We live here on this earth now as strangers and aliens, awaiting a better country that is from above (Hebrews 11:13-16). One day—and it may be very soon—the kingdoms of this world will be overcome and obliterated by the Kingdom of our God

(Revelation 11:15). Our mission is to live as if that day were here and now, and to "occupy until He comes." (Luke 19:13).

Life under the rule and reign of our King is better by far than anything anyone could ever imagine. It's a way of life that can never be duplicated under any other system of human government.

No matter how good other leaders may be, no one compares to Jesus. So, we pledge allegiance to Him. We cannot serve two masters.

CHAPTER 2

A MATTER OF PERSPECTIVE

"It must be noted that Jesus alone reveals who God is. We cannot deduce anything about Jesus from what we think we know about God; however, we must deduce everything about God from what we know about Jesus."

– BRENNAN MANNING[1]

Before we go much further it's probably a good idea for me to explain the way I look at the Scriptures, because it is very likely that it is not the same way that you look at those same scriptures. If nothing else, you will understand why I arrive at the conclusions I do, and why your mileage and mine may vary.

The way I view Scripture is very Jesus-centric. That means I view all of Scripture through the lens of Jesus. To me, Jesus, the Head of the Church, is the ultimate and final authority on God's Word. In fact, as we all know from the first chapter of John's Gospel, He is the "Word of God" who was "made flesh and dwelt among us." Therefore, Jesus is the plumb line with which everything else must align.

But this is not the view of the majority of Christians today. Instead, most evangelicals tend to adopt a "Flat Bible" approach which views the Old Covenant Scriptures and the New Covenant Scriptures on equal terms. Those who embrace this view tend to focus more on the writings of Moses (in the Old Testament) and Paul (in the New Testament). They usually do not accept the idea that a Christian can actually put the commands of Jesus into practice. They often over-emphasize man's sinful nature and view man as being utterly helpless when it comes to things like loving their enemies, turning the other cheek, and blessing those who curse you.

Because of this, many "Flat Bible" Christians tend to downgrade the teachings of Jesus, especially the Sermon on the Mount, and see most of His commands as being unattainable in the here and now.

Some even go so far as to say that Jesus' message about the Kingdom was for a future time, after the second coming or in the New Jerusalem.

"Flat Bible" Christians tend to emphasize grace and forgiveness while "Jesus-centric" Christians most often emphasize submission to Christ and daily obedience to Him.

"Jesus-centric" Christians believe that the Gospel is about the Good News of the Kingdom. They believe that being a Christian means following Jesus daily, taking up your cross, and putting the words of Jesus into practice with help from His Spirit. Historically, these sorts of Christians were called "Anabaptists" in the 16th century, for example. They were devoted to a radical reformation that exceeded that of Martin Luther and John Calvin and sought to return the Christian faith to a time where Jesus alone was the final authority and allegiance to Christ was paramount. Much like what Christians in the early church practiced as they moved away from a strict observance of Old Covenant scriptures—as evidenced in the Apostle Paul's fierce opposition to the "Judaizers" of his day—in favor of a Messianic New Covenant reality.

As a result, "Jesus-centric" Christians also believe that the New Testament is more authoritative than the rest of the Bible. They believe that while the Old Covenant scriptures pointed to Christ, the New Covenant scriptures are the final and complete revelation of Christ.[2]

Many "Flat Bible" Christians want to argue that "all scripture is equally authoritative" and often point to 2 Timothy 3:16-17 which says:

> "All Scripture is God-breathed and is useful for teaching, rebuking, correcting and training in righteousness, so that the servant of God may be thoroughly equipped for every good work."

In rebuttal, a "Jesus-centric" Christian would say that the scriptures are certainly useful for exactly these reasons, but that not every part of scripture is equally authoritative. One might also point out that even "Flat Bible" Christians do not actually believe that all scriptures are equally authoritative as they do not themselves observe Jewish festivals, greet one another with a holy kiss, avoid eating pork and shellfish, or stone people to death for breaking one of the Ten Commandments. So, in this area both sides are in agreement: All scripture is *not* equally authoritative.

What disagreements there may be between the two viewpoints are rooted more in the realm of which scriptures are held as authoritative and which are not. For "Jesus-centric" Christians everything is filtered through the lens of Christ as He is the "Word made flesh."

"Jesus-centric" Christians also believe that in Christ we have the best and clearest picture of who God is and of what God wants.

As Paul said, "...for to this day the same veil remains when the old covenant is read. It has not been removed, because only in Christ is it taken away" (2 Corinthians 3:13-15).

Simply put, Jesus reveals the Father to us. When we have seen Jesus, we have seen the Father (John 14). This means that God the Father is like Jesus. He has always been like Jesus.

Jesus is not what God the Father looks like on a good day. Jesus is what God looks like after He has been beaten, tortured, mocked, spit on, and nailed to a cross to hang for six hours.[3]

JESUS IS NOT WHAT GOD THE FATHER LOOKS LIKE ON A GOOD DAY. JESUS IS WHAT GOD LOOKS LIKE AFTER HE HAS BEEN BEATEN, TORTURED, MOCKED, SPIT ON, AND NAILED TO A CROSS TO HANG FOR SIX HOURS.

Those who take a "Flat Bible" approach tend to have a faith that most closely resembles the Jewish faith. For example, other than the Old Covenant ceremonial and dietary laws, many "Flat Bible" Christians still believe in following the Old Testament scriptures. This means that, for many of them, accumulating wealth, participating in war, and divorce are acceptable behaviors for Christians, simply because they are allowed in the Old Covenant scriptures.

They are also most likely to point to those Old Testament passages and proclaim "God doesn't change!" as a justification for such behaviors.

For those who are "Jesus-centric," the teachings of Jesus on these matters—accumulating wealth, participating in war, divorce and remarriage—are the only standard they follow. So, for them these behaviors are not acceptable as they are forbidden by Christ who gave many teachings against the love of money, and said that His disciples should give up all that they have to follow Him, and said that our enemies should be loved, not opposed with violence, etc.

Finally, those who take a "Jesus-centric" approach believe the words of Jesus can actually be followed, and are meant to be obeyed, not merely quoted, memorized or preached. Yes, many "Flat-Bible" Christians will also affirm this notion, but due to their approach many of them tend to place less of an emphasis on non-violence, loving enemies, and putting the Sermon on the Mount into daily practice.

Historically, Christians who practiced this "Jesus-centric" approach to Scripture (like the Anabaptists) suffered great persecution. They were tortured, imprisoned, and put to death by Christians who embraced the Flat Bible perspective. Many historians readily admit that it was their perspective on the Scriptures that made it acceptable for these Christians to treat their brothers and sisters this way.[4]

So, if you've ever wondered why Evangelicals today can justify support for torture, war, violence, militarism, and nationalism it is simply because they can appeal to Moses and the Old Covenant scriptures as examples of why these are acceptable. They can do so without feeling contradicted by Jesus in the New Covenant simply because their view is "Biblical," even if it might not be specifically "Christian."

Frankly, as I have studied the Anabaptists and their persecution under the Reformed Church in the 16th century, I see many disturbing parallels to our situation today.

We will explore these more as we continue along, but at least now you should have a basic understanding of the way I view the Scriptures—and the way I view life in general—as coming from a Jesus-centric framework.

So, if my views and yours don't line up it is largely due to the fact that I am looking at everything through the lens of Christ, and not through the entire Bible. I try to process the Old

Covenant scriptures through the lens of Christ, not the other way around. Let me take some time to explain why.

At the Mount of Transfiguration there is an astounding lesson for us—one that most Christians completely miss, I'm afraid. There, on the Mount, Jesus and His disciples—Peter, James and John—are suddenly joined by Moses (who stands for the Law) and Elijah (who stands for the Prophets). In that moment, Peter mistakenly attempts to honor all of them together by suggesting that they build three altars: one for Moses, one for Elijah and one for Jesus. What happens next is the lesson we need to learn. The Father responds to Peter's attempt to honor Jesus by removing Moses and Elijah completely. Then the Father speaks from the cloud and says, "This is my Son. Listen to Him!"

Peter wanted to promote Jesus to the status of Moses and Elijah. He thought he was doing Jesus a favor by elevating him to stand alongside such giants of the faith. But in his attempt to elevate Jesus, he was actually demoting the Son of God. That's what he didn't realize, and it is what Christians today don't realize they are doing when they hold the Law (Moses) and the Prophets (Elijah) on the same level as Jesus (God in the flesh).

The Father's response was quick and unmistakable: He removed the Law and the Prophets and left behind only the Son, commanding us to "Listen to Him!"

Does that mean we toss out our Old Covenant Scriptures? Of course not. But it does mean that we don't attempt to place those Old Covenant scriptures on the same level as Jesus. He—and He alone—is our standard and our plumb line.

The pictures of God we have before Christ are wonderful, but they are not in complete focus. Jesus brings those into focus for us like no one else. The prophets of the Old Covenant gave us a wonderful portrait of God, but Jesus is the flesh–and-blood reality.

Like a compass that has pointed us in the right direction and helped to guide us to our ultimate destination, the Old Covenant Scriptures have led us to Jesus. Now that we have Christ living within us, we no longer need to refer to the compass. He is our Good Shepherd. He abides in us, and we abide in Him.

Peter tells us that even the Prophets themselves didn't know what they were writing about, and that only now through Christ do we understand what those Old Covenant scriptures mean.

> "Concerning this salvation, the prophets, who spoke of the grace that was to come to you, searched intently and with the greatest care, trying to find out the time and circumstances to which the Spirit of Christ in them was pointing when he predicted the sufferings of the Messiah and the glories that would follow. It was revealed to them that they were not serving themselves but you, when they spoke of the things that have now been told you by those who have preached the gospel to you by the Holy Spirit sent from heaven. Even angels long to look into these things" (1 Peter 1:10-12).

This is also why Jesus, after he had risen from the dead, had to "open (the) understanding" of the disciples so "that they might comprehend the scriptures" (Luke 24:44-45).

So, what does all this mean? It means that we, as followers of Jesus, need to interpret the Old Covenant (Ten Commandments, Mosaic Laws, etc) through the lens of Christ, not the other way around.

IT MEANS THAT WE, AS FOLLOWERS OF JESUS, NEED TO INTERPRET THE OLD COVENANT (TEN COMMANDMENTS, MOSAIC LAWS, ETC) THROUGH THE LENS OF CHRIST, NOT THE OTHER WAY AROUND.

In other words, we should never take the words of Jesus and filter them through the Old Covenant scriptures. Jesus is the One to whom we are to listen. Jesus outranks Moses. The Sermon on the Mount supplants the Law.

The New Covenant has replaced the Old Covenant which, as the writer of Hebrews tells us, is "obsolete" and "fading away" (Hebrews 8:13).

But, you might ask, how can the Old Covenant be obsolete if Jesus said:

> "Do not think that I have come to abolish the Law or the Prophets; I have not come to abolish them but to fulfill them. I tell you the truth, until heaven and earth disappear, not the smallest letter, not the least stroke of a pen, will by any means disappear from the Law until everything is accomplished" (Matthew 5:17-18).

Notice, there are two qualifiers here: One is that the Law will not disappear "until Heaven and Earth disappear," and the second qualifier is that the Law will not disappear until "everything is accomplished."

So, first Jesus assures us that His mission is to fulfill or to accomplish the Law, and then He tells us that the Law will not disappear "until everything is accomplished."

The question is: "Was everything accomplished?"

And the answer is: Yes!

"When he had received the drink, Jesus said, 'It is finished.' With that, he bowed his head and gave up his spirit" (John 19:30).

The Greek word Jesus used here for "finished" is literally the word "accomplished." Jesus affirmed to us that he really did accomplish everything he set out to do when he prayed to the Father and said, "I glorified you on earth, having accomplished the work that you gave me to do" (John 17:4).

So here, and on the cross, Jesus declares that He has accomplished His mission to "fulfill the Law," just as He set out to do.

What does that mean, then, according to the two qualifiers Jesus placed on the Law? It means that since everything has been accomplished, the Law has now fulfilled its purpose.

Maybe this is why the Apostle Paul told us that, on the cross, Jesus actually *did* "abolish the Law" by fulfilling (or "accomplishing") it:

> "For He Himself is our peace, who made both groups into one, and broke down the barrier of the dividing wall, by abolishing in His flesh the enmity, which is the Law of commandments contained in ordinances, that in Himself He might make the two into one new man, thus establishing peace" (Ephesians 2:15).

Elsewhere, Paul also affirms for us that "Christ is the *end* of the law" (Romans 10:4). Paul also explains for us the differences between the Old Covenant and the New Covenant—not once but twice.

The first time, in 2 Corinthians, Paul contrasts the Old and the New Covenant, saying:

> "Now if the ministry that brought death, which was engraved in letters on stone, [that's the Old Covenant] came with glory, so that the Israelites could not look steadily at the face of Moses because of its glory, fading though it was, [the Old was "fading"] will not the ministry of the Spirit [that's the New Covenant] be even more glorious?"
>
> "If the ministry that condemns men [the Old] is glorious, how much more glorious is the ministry that brings righteousness! [That's the New.] For what was glorious [the Old] has no glory now in comparison with the surpassing glory. And if what was fading away [the Old] came with glory, how much greater is the glory of that which lasts [the New]!" (2 Corinthians 3:7-11, bracketed additions mine).

So, here Paul tells us the following about the Old Covenant:

- It brought death
- Its glory was fading
- It condemns men
- It *was* glorious (past tense)

- It now has no glory
- It is fading away

However, the New Covenant, in contrast:

- Is more glorious than the Old Covenant
- Brings righteousness
- Has a glory that is surpassing
- Is everlasting

The second contrast and comparison that Paul makes between the Old and the New Covenant is mentioned twice in Galatians:

> "The women (Hagar and Sarah) represent two covenants. One covenant is from Mount Sinai and bears children who are to be slaves: This is Hagar. Now Hagar stands for Mount Sinai in Arabia and corresponds to the present city of Jerusalem, because she is in slavery with her children. But the Jerusalem that is above is free, and she is our mother" (Galatians 4:24-26).

> "But what does Scripture say? "Get rid of the slave woman and her son, for the slave woman's son will never share in the inheritance with the free woman's son." Therefore, brothers and sisters, we are not children of the slave woman, but of the free woman" (Galatians 4:30-31).

Now what does Paul say about the Old Covenant? The Old Covenant:

- Is from Mount Sinai (where the Ten Commandments were given)
- Bears children who are slaves
- Corresponds to the earthly Jerusalem
- Is in slavery with her children

- Should be cast out of our presence
- Will not share in the inheritance of Christ
- Is not our mother

On the other hand, Paul says that the New Covenant:

- Bears children who are free
- Is of the heavenly New Jerusalem
- Is our true mother
- Shares in the inheritance of Christ

Paul reiterates this point a number of times in his writings:

- "We are not under the law" (Galatians 5:18)
- "We are dead to the law" (Romans 7:4)
- "We are delivered from the law" (Romans 7:6)

Therefore, those who are in Christ are not under the Ten Commandments but under the "Law of Christ," as Paul says, "Carry each other's burdens, and in this way you will fulfill the law of Christ." (Galatians 6:2)

But what about the Jewish people, then? Aren't they God's chosen people?

That depends on what you mean by "Israel" and "chosen". Paul pointed out to us that not everyone who claims to be "Israel" is actually truly "Israel" in God's eyes.

"For not all who are descended from Israel are Israel. Nor because they are his descendants are they all Abraham's children" (Romans 9:6).

John the Baptist said the same thing to the Pharisees who wanted to claim that they were "children of Abraham" (or

"Israel") and therefore blessed and favored of God. He said to them:

> "And do not think you can say to yourselves, 'We have Abraham as our father.' I tell you that out of these stones God can raise up children for Abraham. The ax is already at the root of the trees, and every tree that does not produce good fruit will be cut down and thrown into the fire" (Matthew 3:9-10).

So, the true "Israel of God" is actually found in Galatians where Paul assures us that, "If you belong to Christ, then you are Abraham's seed, and heirs according to the promise" (Galatians 3:29).

Where does that leave the unbelieving Jewish people? The answer is troubling, and it should give us sincere pause and cause us to fall on our knees and cry out to God for their salvation.

Consider this:

> "Who is the liar? It is whoever denies that Jesus is the Christ. Such a person is the antichrist—denying the Father and the Son" (1 John 2:22).

The Jewish people today who deny that Jesus is the Messiah have neither the Father nor the Son. They, like anyone else who rejects Christ, are lost without Him.

Who, then, are God's "chosen" people? Consider what the Apostle Peter says about the Christians he writes to in his first epistle:

> "But you are a chosen people, a royal priesthood, a holy nation, God's special possession, that you may declare the praises of him who called you out of darkness into his wonderful light" (1 Peter 2:9-10).

Who, then, is the true "Israel of God" (Gal 6:16) according to the New Testament? *Anyone who is in Christ.* Who are the "chosen people" of God? *Those who put their hope in Jesus as their Lord and King.*

Let's go back and look at what the Jewish people were "chosen" for in the first place. Were they chosen to be saved? No, because salvation depends upon trust in Christ as Lord and Savior.

What we find is that God chose the Jews to "be a light unto the nations" (Isaiah 49:6), to exemplify their covenant with God, and, especially to be the people group from whom the Messiah would be born.

So, since Jesus was the Messiah and He has already fulfilled the terms of the Old Covenant, the Jewish people have fulfilled their calling. There's nothing more for them to be "chosen" for.

Christians, according to Peter, are now the "chosen of God" to carry the message of the Gospel to every nation. This is our calling as God's "chosen people."

Some "Flat Bible" Christians might claim that the Ten Commandments are still relevant for us today. But according to the very same Bible, this is not the case.

SOME "FLAT BIBLE" CHRISTIANS MIGHT CLAIM THAT THE TEN COMMANDMENTS ARE STILL RELEVANT FOR US TODAY. BUT ACCORDING TO THE VERY SAME BIBLE, THIS IS NOT THE CASE.

The Ten Commandments were the terms of the Old Covenant (which is obsolete and vanishing).

> "Moses was there with the Lord forty days and forty nights without eating bread or drinking water. And he wrote on the tablets the words of the covenant—the Ten Commandments" (Exodus 34:28).

> "He declared to you his covenant, the Ten Commandments, which he commanded you to follow and then wrote them on two stone tablets" (Deuteronomy 4:13).

The Ten Commandments are only mentioned (by name) three times in the entire Bible: in the two Scriptures referenced above, and also in Deuteronomy 10:4. But in each reference, it is clear that God gave the Ten Commandments to the Jews as a Covenant. (Note: There are several other terms used to reference the Ten Commandments, such as "tablets of stone," "stone tables," etc.)

Also, the Ten Commandments were a covenant between God and the nation of Israel, not between God and the entire world:

> "Then the Lord said to Moses, "Write down these words, for in accordance with these words I have made a covenant with you and with Israel" (Exodus 34:27).

Without this covenant, the Jewish people had no basis for being called a nation.[5] If this covenant was in force, then they would have a claim to the promises included in the covenant. However, if they broke this covenant, then they would lose their status as God's chosen people and their status as a nation.

> "Now if you obey me fully and keep my covenant, then out of all nations you will be my treasured possession. Although the whole earth is mine, you will be for me a kingdom of priests and a holy nation.' These are the words you are to speak to the Israelites" (Exodus 19:5-6).

In much the same way that the Constitution is a document that outlines the laws of our nation and establishes our system of government, the Ten Commandments (or the Law) outlines God's terms for establishing the nation state of Israel.

The terms of Israel's nationhood are dependent upon a few things. First, it says, "If you obey me and keep my covenant, *then* you will be my treasured possession."

That's a conditional covenant. We know that the history of Israel records their continual disobedience to God and to His covenant. Because they broke their covenant with God, they were scattered over and over again, until finally the nation of Israel was judged in AD 70 during the destruction of Jerusalem by the Romans—as Jesus predicted it would be in Luke 21, and in the parable of the vineyard (Matthew 21:33-46).

Did you know that the promises connected to the Old Covenant have now been offered unconditionally to those who are under the New Covenant?

It's true! The very same conditional covenant terms spoken to the Jews are repeated in the New Testament as being unconditionally applied to the Church:

> "As you come to him, the living Stone—rejected by men but chosen by God and precious to Him—you also, like living stones, are being built into a spiritual house to be a holy priesthood, offering spiritual sacrifices acceptable to God through Jesus Christ" (1 Peter 2:4-5).

> "But you are a chosen people, a royal priesthood, a holy nation, God's special possession, that you may declare the praises of Him who called you out of darkness into his wonderful light. Once you were not a people, but now you are the people of God; once you had not received mercy, but now you have received mercy" (1 Peter 2:9-10).

Here, Peter declares that Christians "*are* a chosen people, a royal priesthood, a holy nation, God's special possession…" The very same conditional promises originally offered to the Jewish nation in Exodus 19:5-6 are now spoken to the Church as having been fulfilled. So now anyone who is currently found in Christ is the recipient of these promises: to be chosen; to be part of the royal priesthood; to be considered a holy nation and God's special possession. We are also now to be called the people of God, and we are to receive mercy. So, the only condition applied now, under the new covenant, is to be "in Christ". If you are in Christ—who is the "Chosen One" of God—then you may partake in the same promises that have been attributed to Christ. Some Christians mistakenly apply the promises to ethnic Israel, rather than to Christ Himself. This error is fairly recent, having been largely popularized by John Nelson Darby in the 1830s. In America this doctrine (known as Dispensationalism) has become the dominant theology for most mainstream Christian denominations.[6]

However, the good news is that Jesus first came and fulfilled the terms of the Old Covenant. Then, He made a New Covenant with anyone who would receive Him as Lord and Savior.

> "I will put my law in their minds and write it on their hearts. I will be their God and they will be my people… and they will all know me from the least to the greatest for I will remember their sins no more." (Jeremiah 31:33-34 and Hebrews 8:7-9).

We are now under one Covenant, not two. The first has been fulfilled and is now obsolete:

> "In speaking of a new covenant, he makes the first one obsolete. And what is becoming obsolete and growing old is ready to vanish away" (Hebrew 8:13).

Now that we've established the framework for the rest of the book, let's take a look at how the Christian Church arrived at the place it is now.

CHAPTER 3

THE WAY WE WERE: THE CHURCH BEFORE ENTANGLEMENT

"Politics is the church's worst problem. It is her constant temptation, the occasion of her greatest disasters, the trap continually set for her by the prince of this world."

– JACQUES ELLUL

Historically, the early Christian church viewed the State as an adversary—at best a necessary evil—and something that they were to be called out from. They did not see the secular government as something to be embraced or with which to become entangled.

Paul affirmed in Romans 13 that the State served a purpose (to wield the sword and maintain civil authority), but that the Church served a higher purpose: to carry the cross and proclaim the Gospel of the Kingdom.

There was never any question for Paul, or for the early Christian church, that these two functions were divided between the two groups. The Church and the State were separate entities with different goals and radically different ideals.

The early Christian church took all of that to heart. From the earliest writings of the apostles, through the second and third centuries, the Church resisted military involvement and refused engagement at the political level—even requiring new disciples to the faith who already served in public office to resign or else be turned away at the Lord's Table and disqualified from baptism.[1]

They, like the Anabaptists who came after them during the Reformation, took all of their cues from Jesus. They took His words and put them into practice in their daily lives. They saw the Kingdom of God that Jesus came and died to proclaim as something that was here now, not something that might come one day when Jesus returned.

FROM THE EARLIEST WRITINGS OF THE APOSTLES, THROUGH THE SECOND AND THIRD CENTURIES, THE CHURCH RESISTED MILITARY INVOLVEMENT AND REFUSED ENGAGEMENT AT THE POLITICAL LEVEL

Because of this, they saw their faith as something that was actively bringing Christ's Kingdom into this world with each and every demonstration of His rule and reign in their own lives.

This two-kingdom approach was embedded in the DNA of the early church. It resonated throughout their writings. It reverberated through their fellowship. It marked them out as a peculiar people who were radically different from the world around them.

As Christian scholar David Bercot notes:

> "For the early Christians, it wasn't a matter of lip service. It was a stark reality. They truly were citizens of a different kingdom than the people around them and the Romans took note of this—how different, how peculiar these Christians were."[2]

Many of us today might say that we also embrace a similar two-kingdom approach. However, if we are honest, we must admit that what we actually mean is that we take a particular stance on gay marriage or abortion, or that we vote a certain way. This is generally where most of our convictions along these lines end.

But, the lives of the early Christians were radically different and provided a much greater contrast to the lives of those around them. They were counter-cultural in the extreme. They didn't participate in the entertainment of the Romans. They didn't celebrate the arts of the Romans. They refused to attend the games along with everyone else. They took no sides in any political debate or military conflict. They would not allow someone who worked in politics to fellowship with them unless that person renounced their governmental post and resigned.

Which of us could say the same today?

As Bercot again reminds us:

> "When it gets down to the nitty gritty, most professing Christians today still think that they can mix these two kingdoms together. When push comes to shove, even persons who profess to be Bible-believing Christians, who say that they are no part of this world, act almost no differently than does the world except for a few highly visible issues like abortion, homosexuality, illegal drugs, etc. and because they take a conservative stand on a few issues like that, they delude themselves into thinking they are really different from this world. But the truth is, most professing Christians today are thoroughly part of this world: its government, its mindset, [and] its commercial organizations."[3]

For nearly three hundred years, the Christian church remained defiantly untangled with the Empire. We know this because of the numerous writings we have from several of those early Christian teachers who regularly tried to explain to the Romans why they did not engage in politics.

As Tertullian wrote to the Romans around the year 195:

> "In us, all zeal in the pursuit of glory and honor is dead. So we have no pressing inducement to take part in your public

> meetings, nor is there anything more entirely foreign to us than the affairs of State."

Origen also wrote to Celsus in an attempt to explain the peculiar Christian practice of noninvolvement with Roman politics, saying:

> "It is not for the purpose of escaping public duties that Christians decline public offices, but that they may reserve themselves for a diviner and more necessary service in the Church of God—for the salvation of men. And this service is at once necessary and right."

He also explains to Celsus that those who follow Christ recognize another, higher authority than the State; and that, because of this, they urge their best and brightest to apply their wisdom, talents, and qualities of leadership to further the more urgent and necessary work of the Kingdom of God. He wrote:

> "We recognize in each state the existence of another national organization [the Church], founded by the Word of God, and we exhort those who are mighty in word and of blameless life to rule over Churches. Those who are ambitious of ruling we reject; but we constrain those who, through excess of modesty, are not easily induced to take a public charge in the Church of God. And those who rule over us well are under the constraining influence of the great King, whom we believe to be the Son of God, God the Word. And if those who govern in the Church, and are called rulers of the divine nation—that is, the Church—rule well, they rule in accordance with the divine commands, and never suffer themselves to be led astray by worldly policy."

To Origen, and Tertullian, and every other Christian in those first 300 years of the Untangled Church, the issue was clear and the differences were distinct: Those who were citizens of the Kingdom of God were uninterested in the kingdoms of men. Not that they didn't care about the people who lived within those worldly kingdoms, but their focus was on living for Christ's Kingdom and wooing others to do the same.

They did so by loving them, serving them, and sharing the love of Christ with them—even when they were persecuted, arrested, beaten, or put to death in the process.

But at no time in those first three centuries did those same Christians ever look to gain power within the Roman government as a means to change the world, spread the Gospel, or lessen their own sufferings.

One compelling reason was undoubtedly because when Satan offered Jesus the opportunity to advance the Kingdom of God by wielding political power over the nations, he refused. Such a temptation was from the Evil one.

Instead of pursuing political power, Jesus embraced the cross and in so doing abandoned the sword of worldly governments.

IF JESUS COULD NOT BOW DOWN AND WORSHIP SATAN BY ENTERING PUBLIC OFFICE, PERHAPS WE SHOULDN'T EITHER.

Make no mistake, those early Christians were following the example of Jesus. They did so at great personal cost. Jesus did not involve himself in the politics of his day. As we are told in John 6:15, "Jesus, knowing that they intended to come and make him king by force, withdrew again to a mountain by himself."

Was Jesus neglecting his duties? Couldn't he have made an excellent impact on the Roman Empire if he had entered public office? Many Christians today would argue that Jesus missed an opportunity here, but it was Satan that offered Jesus the Kingdoms of this World, if only He would bow down and worship.

If Jesus could not bow down and worship Satan by entering public office, perhaps we shouldn't either.

As Paul urged us all:

> "Do not be unequally yoked together with unbelievers. For what fellowship has righteousness with lawlessness? And what communion has light with darkness? Come out from among them

> and be separate, says the Lord. Do not touch what is unclean, and I will receive you" (2 Corinthians 6:14-17).

This is not a verse about marriage, as it is often typically applied. No, here Paul warns us not to be entangled with the ways of this world. How can a Christian engage in politics without becoming yoked with unbelievers in the process? The answer is, we can't.

So, then, what can we do? We can live here as aliens and strangers as the New Testament Scriptures call us to do: "Dear friends, I urge you, as foreigners and exiles, to abstain from sinful desires, which wage war against your soul" (1 Peter 2:11).

As the writer of Hebrews reminds us, we are "foreigners and strangers on earth" who "are looking for a country of [our] own…a better country—a heavenly one" (Hebrews 11:13-16).

Those early Christians radically embraced this idea with all of their hearts. Taitian, in AD 160, agreed when he said:

> "I do not wish to be a King. I am not anxious to be rich. I decline military command. I detest fornication. I am not impelled by an insatiable love of gain to go to sea. I do not contend for military honors. I am free from a mad thirst for fame. I despise death. Die to the world, repudiating the madness that is in it! Live to God!"

Clement of Alexandria, in 195 AD, said, "We have no country on earth. Therefore, we can disdain earthly possessions."

And Tertullian wrote, in 212 AD:

> "As for you, you are a foreigner in this world, a citizen of Jerusalem, the city above. Our citizenship, the Apostle says, is in heaven. You have your own calendar. You have nothing to do with the joys of this world. In fact, you are called to the very opposite. For the world will rejoice but you will mourn."

And even Cyprian, who himself was slowly beginning to allow his previous pagan ideas of hierarchy to creep into the Church in 250 AD could still say with conviction:

> "We should ever and a day reflect that we have renounced the world and are in the meantime living here as guests and strangers."

What we see when we look back at the Christian church in the first 300 years of history is a uniformity of conviction that the Church and the State were opposite realms, and that to be a citizen of Christ's Kingdom was to be uninvolved in the affairs of the kingdom of this world. They embraced this idea by living under a clear set of values that brought them into near-constant conflict with the world around them. The pagans could not help but notice how different these Christians were. Those Christians could not help but stand out from the crowd by the way they lived their lives in stark contrast to those unbelievers around them.

Of course, all of that began to change around 312 AD when the Emperor Constantine allegedly converted to Christianity. But the form of Christianity that Constantine offered the Church, as we will see in the next chapter, was one that was fused with the State.

CHAPTER 4

HOW WE FIRST BECAME CONFUSED ABOUT WHO WE REALLY ARE

"When fascism comes to America it will be wrapped in the flag and carrying a cross."

– SINCLAIR LEWIS

To understand how the Christian Church became entangled with politics and the affairs of the State, we first have to understand the underlying reality of what life was like for Christians in those first three centuries after the death and resurrection of Christ.

To say that it was challenging to follow Christ in those first three hundred years of the faith would be an understatement. Most of those early converts were poor, as were most citizens of occupied Jerusalem and surrounding territories within the Roman Empire. However, most were mentally and emotionally prepared to deal with the challenges of poverty. They knew they could work with their hands if they had some marketable skill. Voluntary slavery was always an option for those who lacked the education or talent to provide for themselves. But faith in Christ, in those early years, meant an additional hardship: persecution.

At first, opposition came from their own Jewish brethren, as we see in the book of Acts and from the writings of Paul and Peter in the New Testament (as well as in other historical sources).

The persecution of Christians started out with beatings, imprisonment, and a strong warning not to preach in the name of Christ. But with the stoning of Stephen, persecution of Christians took on a darker tone. Many of Jesus' disciples scattered to other territories where the Jewish opposition wasn't as deadly at first.

IRONICALLY, THESE PERSECUTIONS TURNED MARTYRS INTO HEROES, AND THIS IN TURN SPURRED EVEN MORE FOLLOWERS OF CHRIST TO STAND FIRM AND SHARE THEIR LOVE FOR JESUS, DESPITE THE PERSECUTION THEY SUFFERED.

As the years progressed, the amount and ferocity of persecution endured by Christians increased. The Romans had taken notice of the number of Gentile converts being added to the Church, and they began their own brand of persecution against the followers of Christ.

This Roman persecution is what amplified the cost of becoming a Christian in those early centuries. Yet, the increased threats of torture—and the mounting cruelty of such torture—did little to slow the spread of the Gospel. Ironically, these persecutions turned martyrs into heroes, and this in turn spurred even more followers of Christ to stand firm and share their love for Jesus, despite the persecution they suffered.

Under the reign of Nero, the cruelties against the Christians became unbelievably horrific. Those who refused to renounce their faith in Jesus were skinned alive, burned at the stake, and eventually used as an endless source of entertainment in the arena, as Roman citizens gleefully cheered while Christians were eaten alive by lions or slaughtered by gladiators. Nero even boasted of lighting his garden at night with the bodies of burning Christians who refused deny Christ and proclaim Nero as their Lord.

There were hardly any lukewarm Christians in those dark seasons of Church history. Anyone who received the Gospel and made the decision to be baptized under the name of Jesus knew full well that their life was truly being laid on the altar—or upon the cross—as a living sacrifice to Christ. The message was clear: Jesus laid down His life for you, and now you are laying down your life for Him and for your fellow man in Christian love.

One of the most inspiring acts of Christian devotion was recorded in the persecution of Carpus and Papylus. When brought together before the proconsul on suspicion of being Christians, Carpus was asked to renounce Jesus and to sacrifice to the gods as Caesar had commanded all men to do. His response was, "I cannot sacrifice. I have never yet sacrificed to idols." At once the proconsul ordered him to be hung up and had his skin flayed with tools of torture. With each strip of his flesh they removed he cried out "I am a Christian! I am a Christian!" and, after the torture continued a long time, he could no longer speak.

Then the proconsul turned to Papylus and asked him, "Are you also a Christian?"

Now let's imagine for a moment that you were standing there instead of Papylus. You've just witnessed your friend and brother in Christ, Carpus, being flayed alive in front of you. You've heard his defiant declarations of faith in Jesus with every strip of flesh that was ripped from his back. And now you are asked the same question: "Are you also a Christian?"[1]

This question shatters me. I cannot answer right away. I have to close my eyes and take inner stock of my love for Christ. If I am honest, I can say what I would hope to answer in that situation. I would hope that I would have the courage and the faith to answer, as our dear brother Papylus did: "I am a Christian. There is nothing I can say which is greater or more wonderful than this."

Then the proconsul had Papylus also hung up and his body was also flayed with three pairs of iron instruments of torture. He did not utter a sound.

Afterwards they were both ordered to be burned at the stake. They both ran quickly to the wooden stakes that were already prepared for them and they were each nailed there and the fires were set. Papylus remained silent in the flames and quietly gave up his soul to God. Carpus, however, was full of joy and began to pray loudly, "Praise be to thee O Lord, Jesus Christ, son of God, that you have considered me, a sinner, worthy of this part in thee!"

In the crowd of onlookers there was one sister in Christ by the name of Agathonica. When she witnessed the inspired love of Christ put on display by these two brothers, she cried out loudly, "This meal has been prepared for me! I must partake of it. I must receive the meal of glory!" and she joyfully submitted herself to be nailed to a stake and burned alive with them singing, "Lord, Lord, Lord, help me, for I flee to thee!"[2]

This happened in the year 165 AD, and it is quite typical of what Christians in those early years had come to expect as a consequence of following Jesus as Messiah.

The Christian church endured nearly three hundred years' worth of such persecution and cruelty. We can hardly imagine it today. But for millions of our brothers and sisters in Christ, this was all they knew of the faith. There was no other way to live as a disciple of Jesus. The threat of imprisonment, torture, and death were accepted along with the Gospel of Christ as normative for anyone seeking to follow in the footsteps of Jesus.

We must point out that, as horrific as these persecutions were, they served as an unmistakable opportunity for the transforming love of Christ to be put on dramatic display before the entire Empire of Rome. No pagan had any paradigm for the love and devotion these Christ-followers had for Jesus. Not one of them knew how to process this kind of commitment and passion. It simply made no sense, unless this Jesus was exactly who they claimed He was.

The intensity of such persecutions waxed and waned over those three hundred years, but persecution never ceased completely. Not until the Emperor Constantine announced, around 312 AD, that he had seen a vision of Christ and was now a friend of Christians throughout the Roman Empire did persecution cease.

RATHER THAN ATTEMPTING TO WIPE THEM OUT WITH THE SWORD—WHICH HAD PROVEN USELESS OVER A THREE HUNDRED YEAR PERIOD—THE EMPIRE NOW SOUGHT TO ASSIMILATE CHRISTIANITY INTO A MELTING POT OF RELIGIONS AND WIN THEM OVER WITH EXTRAVAGANT KINDNESSES.

For many in the Christian Church, Constantine's announcement was seen as an answer to their prayers. No longer would they have to live in fear. The Emperor was now on their side! What could be better than this?

But for others, this sudden reversal of fortune was a little too convenient. These skeptical Christians, while in the minority, felt that the Empire had not become their friend as much as it had simply altered its strategy against them. Rather than attempting to wipe them out with the sword—which had proven useless over a three hundred year period—the Empire now sought to assimilate Christianity into a melting pot of religions and win them over with extravagant kindnesses.

The spurious nature of Constantine's conversion experience added to their doubts about the Emperor's sincerity. As Eusebius, a Christian historian who was under the employ of Constantine and served in his royal court, reports the story, Constantine was about to enter into battle at the Milvian Bridge in Italy. The day before the conflict, Constantine claims to have seen a vision of a cross in the sky above the noon-day sun and hearing the words "Conquer with this" being spoken to him, presumably by God. That night he had a dream of Jesus appearing to him. In the dream, he was commanded to make a replica of the sign, and to use it as a symbol of protection in his battle the next day.

Eusebius reports that, at that time, "[Constantine] resolved to worship none but the God who had been revealed to him."[3]

History tells us that Constantine did, in fact, win that battle at the Milvian Bridge, and that he attributed his bloody victory to the power of Christ and the symbol which was given to him in the vision and dream. But what exactly that symbol may have actually been is confusing, because it was not the simple cross that Constantine actually adopted as his symbol but the Chi-Rho, which resembled an Egyptian ankh and contained the first two letters of the name "Christos" at the top of a cross and which he called the "Labarum." It became, in the words of one Constantinian scholar, "a magical, miraculous amulet, almost equivalent to the Ark of the Covenant."[4]

Beyond the sketchy details of Constantine's conversion experience, we also might question the validity of his faith in Christ once we learn that he took no interest in the actual life or teachings of Jesus at all, and that he "also rebuked his half-sister Constantia for excessively revering what was believed to be a likeness of Jesus."[5] Constantine saw the cross more as an emblem of military power than as a symbol of Christ's suffering or death.

We might also recoil with the knowledge that Constantine, after his supposed conversion to faith in Christ, had his own son and his wife put to death on questionable pretenses and that "historians point out that even after this event [his conversion] Constantine continued worshipping the Unconquered Son [Apollo]."[6]

Constantine's conversion was handled quite differently by the Christian Church than any other person's. He was not put through the long process of discipline and instruction in the teachings of Christ as most new converts were.

According to New Testament scholar, Justo Gonzalez:

> "Throughout his entire life, he [Constantine] never placed himself under the direction of Christian teachers or bishops... Constantine reserved the right to determine his own religious practices, and even to intervene in the life of the church, for he considered himself "the bishop of bishops." Repeatedly, even after his conversion, he took part in pagan rites in which no Christian would participate, and the bishops raised no voice of condemnation."[7]

He was also never baptized into the faith, as every other Christian disciple was expected to do, and only submitted to baptism on his deathbed.

Yet, in spite of all of this, many Christians embraced Constantine and his self-pronounced Christian faith. Why? Partially because—whether legitimate or not—his conversion meant for them the end to hundreds of years of horrific persecution.

But that wasn't the only reason for their willingness to accept Constantine's olive branch. Along with the ceasing of persecutions, Constantine offered the Christian church—and especially their leaders—a place of great honor and respectability within the Empire. Bishops were placed on the payroll and granted tax-exempt status. Pagan temples were converted and handed over to Christians for use in public worship. In some cases, elaborate

Christian temples were constructed by Constantine to allow for the expansion of the faith throughout the Empire.

So, in exchange for a place of honor and acceptability within the public square, the Christian Church sold her birthright and bowed her knees to the State.

It's very much like the scene in the film, *It's A Wonderful Life,* where George Bailey is called into the office of Old Man Potter. Potter has tried for years to grab up every bit of property and power in the little town of Bedford Falls. Only one man has stood up to him and prevented him from having his way, and that man is George Bailey. Bailey is a quiet, humble, yet principled young man who sees through Potter's schemes and opposes him at every turn.

After years of trying his best to beat Bailey, Old Man Potter tries a different approach. He summons Bailey into his office. He offers him a seat and hands him an expensive cigar. Then he begins to shower Bailey with compliments, praising him for his resourcefulness, and subtly reminding him of how little he has received in return for his quiet heroism against injustice. Finally, Potter springs his trap and says, "You've beaten me, George." Then he offers Bailey a contract paying double the salary he's currently earning.

In the film, you can see Bailey's mind churning with the allure of Potter's offer. He has always wanted to travel and see the world. This offer would make that possible. He has children to care for, and this opportunity would allow him to provide in abundance for his wife and his growing family.

He is intrigued by the offer; yet, he is wise enough to ask for time to talk it over with his wife. Potter agrees and then something happens when Bailey shakes Potter's hand. We can see it on his face as he pulls his hand back and then wipes it on his shirt. He realizes that he is being manipulated by Potter and that this is only another scheme of Potter's to take control of little Bedford Falls, once and for all.

In the film, Bailey refuses the offer. But in our analogy, when the Church is offered an opportunity to receive a respectable place in the community, tax exemptions, and ornate buildings in exchange for her allegiance to the State, she gladly accepts it.

Even more insidious was Constantine's redefining of the Christian faith from within. As we saw in our previous chapter, the person who dared to take the name of "Christian" was one who was prepared to put the teachings of Christ into practice in their daily life - even to the point of death if necessary. But now, under Constantine, the definition of a Christian was about to be redefined as one who accepted the basic doctrines of the faith, regardless of how one might live their life day-to-day.

New Testament scholar Justo Gonzalez notes:

> "Constantine's impact on the life of the church was such that it was still felt as late as the twentieth century. But there were also more immediate consequences of his reign and policies, changes in the life of the church that became apparent almost immediately...One of the results of the new situation was the development of what may be called an 'official theology.'"[8]

On one level, we can hardly blame Christians during this time for being overwhelmed by the Emperor's graciousness towards them. To them it must have seemed like a miracle; but, in their stupor, they quickly handed him the keys to their faith and did what no other Christian would have ever done: they bowed their knees and swore allegiance to the Emperor and the Roman Empire.

Once Constantine had won the admiration and trust of many Christian leaders in the Church, he used that influence to oversee the codification of Christian theology into a set of doctrines that would now define who was truly "Christian" and who was not.

Armed with these documents, the Church very quickly began to persecute their own brothers and sisters who disagreed with these new official statements of faith.

IRONICALLY ENOUGH, THE CHURCH COMPROMISED HER VALUES SO THAT THE SWORD WOULD NO LONGER COME AGAINST HER. YET ONCE CONSTANTINE AND THE EMPIRE BECOME ENTANGLED WITH THE CHURCH, THERE WERE EVEN MORE CHRISTIANS BEING PUT TO DEATH THAN EVER BEFORE.

Ironically enough, the Church compromised her values so that the sword would no longer come against her. Yet once Constantine and the Empire become entangled with the Church, there were even more Christians being put to death than ever before. Only now, sadly, it would be the Church itself who would imprison, torture, and even kill any Christian that opposed her—or who opposed the State.

Not every Christian leader in Constantine's day was so willing to play along. For these dissenting few,

> "the fact that the emperors declared themselves Christian…was not a blessing, but rather a great apostasy. Some who tended to look at matters in this light…withdrew to the desert, there to lead a life of meditation and asceticism…The fourth century thus witnessed a massive exodus of devoted Christians to the deserts of Egypt and Syria."[9]

Constantine's influence on the Church produced two major changes: hierarchy and entanglement.

> "Until Constantine's time, Christian worship had been relatively simple. At first Christians gathered to worship in private homes. They began to gather in cemeteries, such as the Roman catacombs... After Constantine's conversion, Christian worship began to be influenced by imperial protocol…Eventually the congregation came to have a less active role in worship."[10]

Under Constantine, the Christian Church began to dispose of notions like the "priesthood of all believers"—where every Christian was seen as a contributive member of the Body of Christ—and adopted more hierarchical elements of worship, where the Bishop presided over something that closely resembled a regal ceremony, with incense, choirs, great speeches, and elaborate liturgy. This shift became quite a natural process as worship began to take place inside temples which were formerly pagan.

Hierarchy wasn't tolerated in the early church due to Christ's strong admonition to his disciples against such behavior. Jesus points to both a secular and a religious hierarchy and says, *"not so with you."*

He sternly warned his disciples not to "lord it over" one another as the Gentile rulers did:

> "Jesus called them together and said, "You know that those who are regarded as rulers of the Gentiles lord it over them, and their high officials exercise authority over them. Not so with you. Instead, whoever wants to become great among you must be your servant, and whoever wants to be first must be slave of all. For even the Son of Man did not come to be served, but to serve, and to give his life as a ransom for many" (Mark 10:42-45).

Jesus also commanded them not to follow the example of the Jewish leaders, who loved the praise of men and built their own kingdoms to glorify themselves.

> "But you are not to be called 'Rabbi,' for you have one Teacher, and you are all brothers. And do not call anyone on earth 'father,' for you have one Father, and he is in heaven. Nor are you to be called instructors, for you have one Instructor, the Messiah. The greatest among you will be your servant. For those who exalt themselves will be humbled, and those who humble themselves will be exalted" (Matthew 23:8-12).

Sadly, as time progressed, the early church did begin to move towards hierarchy as a way of dealing with church discipline from the top down rather than as Jesus and Paul approached it, from a relational standpoint within the Body itself.

Once Constantine arrived on the scene around 300 AD, there were already several church leaders who were more than open to the introduction of a secular and religious hierarchy.[11]

Nevertheless, in this book, we are more concerned with the political entanglement that Constantine introduced into the Christian church. This error, like the introduction of hierarchy, persists to this very day.

By contrasting the voices and practices of the early church with our own modern churches we can more easily recognize the differences between those who are entangled and those who are not.

As Tertullian once observed in a letter to an unbelieving pagan:

> "Yes, and the Caesars too would have believed on Christ, if either the Caesars had not been necessary for the world, or if Christians could have been Caesars."[12]

For early Christians like Tertullian, the very idea of a Christian Caesar was preposterous. For them, there were clearly two kingdoms; and if one became entangled with the other, then both would cease to perform their intended functions. Even worse, the Christian Church, once entangled with the State, would cease to carry the cross of Christ and begin to wield the sword of Rome. The oppressed would become the oppressor, not only of the weak and the marginalized, but even of other Christians.

Every time this pattern is repeated—whenever the Church becomes wedded to the State – we observe a demonic betrayal of Christ-like values in favor of abhorrent displays of violence and power.

When the Anabaptists stood up and defied the State Church—the Reformed State Church of Calvin and Luther—they were arrested, beaten, tortured, and put to death by other Christians because they wanted a Church that wasn't aligned with the State.

Many Christians today who find themselves drawn to the New Testament model of simple or organic church are quite aware of how Constantine introduced pagan ideas of hierarchy into the Church. They are willing to stand against it and defy the status quo of institutional church. However, not as many of them are willing to admit that this same Constantine introduced an equally heretical practice of entanglement between Church and State.

If we truly understand that the Church went off the rails by aligning herself with Constantine, then it shouldn't be too hard to see that anyone who maintains political entanglements is still emulating that same Constantinian form of Church.

Perhaps part of the problem is that Christians who have left the traditional church are still carrying some of the baggage they brought with them from the Constantinian form of church? Maybe they have yet to fully grasp all that the Constantinian model stands for?

My hope and prayer is that Christians would renounce everything that Constantine introduced to the Church and would return to the words of Jesus for instruction, wisdom and guidance.

What would have happened if George Bailey had accepted Potter's offer? We get a glimpse of that later in the film when George Bailey is allowed to see what life would have been like had he never lived. His influence on the town was significant. In his vision he finds that Bedford Falls has become Pottersville, a dark, violent, seedy town filled with crime and oppression. This is the town without George Bailey's loving, self-sacrificing stand against Potter's greedy schemes. It's a nightmare.

Sadly, we have a similar vantage point. We get to look back through time and see what the Church was like immediately after the influence of Jesus and the Apostles. In the three hundred years that followed, we see a people who were devoted to Christ, sold out to the Gospel of the Kingdom, and willing to lay down their lives for the Truth.

We also get to see what the world would be like if those Christians had pledged allegiance to the State and aligned herself with the Empire. In less than a generation, those same Christians who were once put to death under the Roman sword were soon wielding the sword to put to death their own brothers and sisters in Christ.

The oppressed had become the oppressor. The free had become the entangled. Those marked by love had now become marked by violence.

This is how we became entangled with the State. Now, let's examine the fruit of that entanglement.

CHAPTER 5

THE WEAKNESS OF POLITICS AS AN AGENT OF CHANGE

"If you ever injected truth into politics you would have no politics."

– WILL ROGERS

Our attention so far has been centered on the words of Jesus, the writings of the Apostles, and early Church history. But now I'd like to take a slightly different approach. Let's turn our attention to the other side of our coin: politics.

For many American Christians, the idea of separating their faith and their politics is absurd. They see nothing wrong with having an American flag in the sanctuary. They have no problem pledging allegiance to the flag before the service starts. They sincerely believe that being patriotic and Christian is perfectly fine, even normal.

But let me ask you this: In over 6,000 years of human history, how many of mankind's basic problems have been solved by politicians? How many of man's sins have been dealt with by even the greatest politicians who have ever lived?

If we're honest, our political process is largely incapable of bringing about the fundamental transformation necessary to improve our condition, with very few exceptions.

As stewards who must one day give an account of our money and time, why would we invest anything in a system with such a disappointing track record for success?

Of course, politics were never designed to "change the world." Politics are essentially about writing, passing, and enforcing laws. But we know from Scripture that even God's Law wasn't capable of transforming the hearts of men and women. Why do we still believe that we can do any better?

Do we really need more laws? Do we need better people writing the laws? Is our problem the lack of law enforcement?

What does the Bible have to say about all of that? Do experts in the Law set us free? Is the Law capable of changing us into the image of God?

"For if righteousness comes through the law, then Christ died for no purpose" (Galatians. 2:21).

Now, let me ask you this: What if there was something that could reform the convict? What if there was a formula for changing people into better citizens? What if there was hope for every broken marriage? What if every addict could find hope for life beyond their daily habit? What if there was a way to create an entire society of people who loved one another, cared for one another, and went out of their way to bless everyone around them?

Wouldn't something that revolutionary—something with the power to change every human heart from within and make them a brand new creature –be better than any political solution on the planet? And if—just if—that sort of society-changing paradigm actually existed, wouldn't it be foolish to waste your time on a political solution? Especially if so far not one single politician or political ideology had ever once come close to something nearly as effective and powerful?

Still, many of us cannot break free of the allure of politics and political influence over others. As Christian leader Franklin Graham recently said:

> "Can you imagine what a difference it would make if Christians ran for every office at all levels across our country—city council, school board, Mayor? We need to get involved and take a stand for biblical values and morals before it's too late."[1]

Unfortunately, this quote reflects the attitude of many Christians in America today. It reveals a deep desire to seize control of the American government—to take power over our enemies and to exert the necessary political pressure required to "turn our nation back to God."

Of course, this is always couched in language that suggests that our nation was founded under Christian principles and assumes that if Christians would just vote the "right way" and "take a stand for Biblical values" then our nation would be restored to its original piety.

IT REVEALS A DEEP DESIRE TO SEIZE CONTROL OF THE AMERICAN GOVERNMENT—TO TAKE POWER OVER OUR ENEMIES AND TO EXERT THE NECESSARY POLITICAL PRESSURE REQUIRED TO "TURN OUR NATION BACK TO GOD."

I always wonder how exactly this miracle would take place. As far as I know, no one has ever actually explained the logic of this fantasy.

If every political office in America were filled by a Christian, as Franklin Graham suggests, would some magical shift in the collective consciousness of the American people take place? Would everyone suddenly stop in their tracks and agree that it was time to become moral and righteous?

Honestly, I don't think even Franklin Graham himself actually believes in that scenario. No, I believe the truth is that if

Christians were to eventually seize control of every political office in the land, the proposed cure might be worse than the proverbial disease.

See, for Christians to actually gain power and keep it, they would have to start using that same power to start passing as many "Christian laws" as possible. Once enough of those laws were on the books, then non-Christian people would have no choice but to begin acting more like Christians want them to act. Not because they had new hearts that were transformed from within by the Spirit of God, but because to act otherwise would mean paying a fine or perhaps imprisonment.

Does any of that sound good to you? Hopefully not.

But what's even more ludicrous about Franklin Graham's political fantasy is the idea that a government comprised entirely of Christian politicians would automatically lead to national unity.

This is laughable. Anyone who has ever sat through a Church business meeting could tell you that. Since when do large groups of Christians actually agree on anything?

If you lack evidence for how divided Christians can be on issues, may I suggest you try joining a few Christian groups on Facebook for a week. That should reveal just how foolish this idea of automatic Christian unity over issues really is.

We already know that Christians in the same church can't agree on what color to paint the baptistery. Just imagine a Christian Congress made up of Lutherans, Baptists, Methodists, Charismatics and Pentecostals trying to agree on a rail system or a public school curriculum. Would that improve our political process or diminish it? I think the answer should be obvious.

Even if you don't agree with me on this point, let's at least come together on this one thing: It's not the goal that Jesus has in mind for His people.

Jesus never suggests that His followers should attempt to control people using political means. In fact, it was Satan who offered Jesus that same opportunity during those 40 days in the desert, and Jesus refused to advance His Kingdom by political means. Why in the world would we decide to start giving in to Satan's temptation now?

But what about historical heroes like William Wilberforce or Martin Luther King, Jr.? Weren't these men, and others like them, compelled by their faith in Christ to effect positive change through political means?

This is a valid question, and one I believe we should take time to examine carefully.

William Wilberforce worked tirelessly over a span of three decades to pass the Abolition of Slavery bill in the House of Commons, thereby ending slavery in the British Empire on July 26, 1833. Three days later he died, his life's work complete.

At first blush, Wilberforce's valiant efforts appear to cast serious doubts about my call for Christians to abandon politics. Wasn't it a good thing for Wilberforce to devote himself to abolishing slavery in his home nation? Doesn't that prove that politics can be used by God as a tool for good?

Certainly, no one who follows Christ should argue in favor of slavery or human trafficking. Abolishing the slave trade was indeed a wonderful thing, and Wilberforce's methods were certainly preferable to the bloody civil war fought by Americans a few decades later which eventually set their slaves free.

However, we must understand that politics alone did not abolish slavery throughout the British Empire. It took three decades to accomplish, and it was largely due to a sustained movement made up of the followers of Christ in that nation who ultimately prevailed in transforming the hearts and minds of the people.

Those Christian abolitionists not only fasted and prayed for slavery to end, but they also spoke out and boycotted industries and products created through slave labor. They worked tirelessly to change the hearts and minds of their neighbors about the evils of slavery. Eventually, three decades later, their efforts were successful.

THIS IS HOW MOST ADVANCEMENTS IN SOCIAL CHANGE OCCUR. NOT THROUGH THE LEADERSHIP OF PRESIDENTS OR PARLIAMENTS, BUT FROM THE BOTTOM UP.

This is how most advancements in social change occur. Not through the leadership of presidents or parliaments, but from the bottom up.

As Howard Zinn noted when speaking about the passage of the Constitutional Amendments that ended slavery, gave all people equal rights, and guaranteed equal protection under the law, Congress may have passed these laws, but they did so for a good reason:

> "Why? Not because Lincoln or Congress itself initiated them. They passed those amendments because a great movement against slavery had grown up in the country from the 1830s to the 1860s. A powerful anti-slavery movement which pushed Congress into the Thirteenth, Fourteenth and Fifteenth Amendments. This is a very important thing to keep in mind; that when justice comes and when injustices are remedied, they're not remedied by the initiative of the national government or the politicians. They only respond to the power of social movements. And that's what happened with the relationship between anti-slavery movement and the passage of those amendments."[2]

True progress is made when the people move towards justice. If their vision and passion for truth do not waver, then and only then do political leaders feel compelled to respond. This involves becoming involved in the pursuit of Justice, which may run parallel to politics but is nonetheless quite distinct from mere politics.

This is what Martin Luther King Jr. and Wilberforce understood. They worked to move the hearts of people around them so that the hand of politics might also be moved to act justly. They did not primarily seek to campaign for the election of politicians or to place faith in legislation alone. They knew that laws do not change hearts, and that until hearts become moved to demand justice, there can be no real justice for anyone.

Many are not aware that William Wilberforce himself urged Christians to put their hope in Christ rather than to engage in politics. As he said in his book, *A Practical View of Christianity*:

> "*Let true Christians, then … boldly assert the cause of Christ* in an age when so many are ashamed of Him: *and let them consider as [passed down] on them the important duty* of suspending for a while the fall of their own country, and perhaps, of performing a still more extensive service to society at large; *not by busy interference in politics, in which it cannot but be confessed there is much uncertainty,* but rather by that sure and radical benefit of restoring the influence of religion, and of raising the standard of morality."[3]

Clearly, Wilberforce understood that the role of Christians in society was primarily one of transformative moral influence from within the culture, not as the wielder of political power or influence over the culture.

What's more, Wilberforce worked to improve the living conditions of an oppressed people group who could not speak up for themselves. He advocated for those who were victims of a powerful system which exploited them: a system of which Wilberforce himself was an unwilling member.

Furthermore, as a Christian, he was greatly troubled by how faith and Scripture were being mangled to justify the treatment of human beings who were held against their will and used like animals.

In contrast, Christians today are using political power and influence to protect *themselves*—not to protect an oppressed group of people who have no defense against tyranny and abuse. American Christians are seeking to impact their culture through the legislative power of the State, rather than by actually loving, living, and serving the way Jesus commanded.

Wilberforce fought to set others free. American Christians want to use politics to empower *themselves*. In other words, what we see today is a Church that largely seeks to gain political power and favor for their own selfish interests. What is missing is the Justice component.

So, to compare the selfless, sacrificial work of William Wilberforce to abolish slavery on behalf of an oppressed people with the selfish, fear-based paranoia of today's politicized American Christianity is foolish, and practically obscene.

Wilberforce and Martin Luther King, Jr. did more than vote or push for legislation. They, and others like them, stood up to those who had power. They spoke up for those who had no voice. They defied those who exploited the weak. They spoke out against corporate greed. They endured serious persecution and sometimes even physical violence so that others might enjoy freedom. They risked their reputations, even their lives and livelihood, to make life better for an entire group of people who themselves had little power.

If American Christians would be willing to lay their lives on the line and risk personal injury in defense of the weak, marginalized, and exploited people around them, then we might find cause to equate their political wrangling with the valiant efforts of people like MLK or Wilberforce. Until that day, the lust for political power is the farthest thing possible from the historic abolition of slavery and systemic racism on behalf of the oppressed.

Martin Luther King, Jr. took the words of Jesus seriously. He marched out into the streets, knowing he would be brutally opposed. Out of love for his fellow man, he boldly opposed evil and refused to hate his enemy. Is that what you call politics? I believe we would call that Justice.

The sort of political entanglement the Church finds herself in today is more about advancing the agenda of a specific party, not about helping the weak, the poor, the immigrant, the outcast, the orphan or the widow. Politics as practiced by Martin Luther King, Jr. looked like spending the night in jail, getting spit upon by his enemies, and eventually being assassinated for daring to stand up and speak out. This is not what American Christians mean when they talk about politics.

Instead, the Church has become more interested in helping to elect a certain breed of politician who cares more about corporate interests and protecting the interests of the rich and powerful.

According to the Pew Research Center, 76% of the 91 million Evangelicals in America are White. This means that Evangelical Christians represent a majority demographic which wields more privilege and political power than the marginalized in our culture. Rather than relinquish that power so that those who have so little of it might enjoy an equal share, these same Christians continually seek to grasp even more power for themselves and thereby further marginalize those on the bottom.

Finally, if we look closely, we will find that the very same enemy that fought the hardest against Wilberforce and his efforts to end slavery is today the greatest ally of the politically-entangled, American Christian Church: money-hungry corporations.

Please understand. I'm not suggesting that Corporations have become the ally of the Christian Church. I'm saying that the Church, by entangling Herself with politics, has become unequally yoked with those who primarily control the political system for their own gain: Multi-Billion-Dollar Corporations.

A modern day Wilberforce would fight with his last breath against the entangled Christian Church. He would have been the first to remind us, as he did in his own book, that a Christian's first duty is to "boldly assert the cause of Christ" and to seek to influence society, "not by busy interference in politics," but "by raising the standard of morality."

Yet many Christians today seek to change the world through politics, as if Jesus had no other plan of his own. But Jesus *does* have a plan to change the world. It's a good one. It involves our drawing near to Him on a daily basis and being transformed into people who are like Him. It involves helping people around us to come under His rule and reign to experience the same transformational love that we have known ourselves. It involves helping people change, one at a time, into the kinds of people who will love God and love others no matter what laws are on the books or what the penalties for breaking them happen to be.

This, in fact, is exactly what Jesus came and died to institute: a New Covenant where people are made into new creatures with new natures and new hearts. His mission was to implement a reality where "I will put my laws in their minds and write them on their hearts. I will be their God, and they will be my people" (Hebrews 8:10).

When we abandon this marvelous plan that Jesus gave to us, we betray Him. We lay aside the cross that He commanded us to carry and we take up a sword—a symbol of power over others—as an instrument of change.

What has this ever brought us in the past? A glance at the history books reveals the fruit of this way of thinking, and it isn't pretty. Jesus came and gave us an opportunity to "think differently" about everything. He showed us a better way, if only we will place our trust in Him and begin to put that plan into practice.

What Franklin Graham and others like him want—even if they don't say it in so many words—is a Christian theocracy, plain and simple. Even our Founding Fathers didn't want an America like that. Why would anyone want to re-write the Constitution so radically, especially if they claimed to believe that it was a document inspired by God Himself?

SOME CHRISTIANS ARGUE THAT THE CHURCH IS CAPABLE OF CARRYING BOTH THE SWORD AND THE CROSS TOGETHER. BUT THAT'S NOT WHAT THE SCRIPTURES TELL US.

Whatever else we might say about the Founding Fathers, we must admit that—like it or not—they created a nation that was quite intentionally designed to be one where people from every religion—Islam, Judaism, Christianity, Hinduism, or none of the above—would be free to worship, or not worship, as they desired.

They had already seen the negative effects of State religion upon the liberty and freedoms of men and women back in England and elsewhere around the world. They took great pains to ensure that no such religious controls were introduced into the nation they were founding. They understood that, for liberty to flourish, religion must remain separate from the affairs of State.

Oddly enough, our New Testament agrees with this idea. Paul the Apostle wrote that the Church should carry the cross and live out the example of Christ in Romans 12, and then in Romans 13 he described the function and purpose of the State.

These two entities are never intertwined. They are purposely contrasted from one another.

Some Christians argue that the Church is capable of carrying both the sword and the cross together. But that's not what the Scriptures tell us. It's not what we observe the Christian church doing in the first three hundred years immediately following the introduction of the Gospel.

Paul takes care to remind us that the weapons we fight with are not carnal:

> "The weapons we fight with are not the weapons of the world. On the contrary, they have divine power to demolish strongholds" (2 Corinthians 10:4).

> "Rather, as servants of God we commend ourselves in every way...with weapons of righteousness in the right hand and in the left" (2 Corinthians 6:4-8).

If both our hands are carrying "weapons of righteousness" as Paul describes, then it is impossible for us to carry a sword and a cross at the same time. Our hands should be full doing the works of mercy and righteousness as Jesus commanded us.

We have a mandate from our Lord to seek first His Kingdom. We are called to follow Him and His example. We are compelled to pledge allegiance to Him and His Kingdom alone.

So, let the State wield the sword. Let the Church carry the cross. Let the two of them never change places or merge together.

I believe Franklin Graham, and many others like him, have sadly fallen under the spell of Constantine. They see the culture moving away from God; and, instead of calling the Bride of Christ to take up the cross and lay down their lives for the lost, they reach for the sword and align themselves with the Empire as a way to gain favor and exert political influence over others. It's a mistake, and it's in direct contradiction to what Jesus told us to do.

As one great Christian evangelist wisely observed:

> "It would disturb me if there was a wedding between the religious fundamentalists and the political right. The hard right has no interest in religion except to manipulate it"(Billy Graham).[4]

On this point we would be wise to listen to the evangelist. However, we should be careful not only to avoid entanglement with the "political right" but with the left and the center as well. Both sides are off limits to us. We stand with Christ, not with the political elite.

The allure of power and influence is deceptive. We're all susceptible to it in a variety of ways, myself included.

Several decades ago, I was in a Christian band and I wanted more than anything in the world to get signed to a record deal. Why? Well, what I told myself was that I wanted to get signed so that I could share the Gospel with more people. But eventually I had to admit the truth: I really wanted to get signed to a record deal because I wanted to be famous.

The truth was that if all I really wanted was for more people to hear the Gospel, then our band could simply play in bars and clubs and street corners.

Mixing politics and Christianity is no different. We may tell ourselves that we're doing it because we want our nation to be more "Christian." But if that's what we really want, we should spend more time preaching the Gospel and living out the commands of Jesus in our daily life.

But doing that is difficult. It takes personal, daily sacrifice. It involves abiding in Christ moment-by-moment and trusting Him to change both us and the world around us at the same time.

We know that legislation will never change anyone's heart. We know that the Gospel is not spread through political initiatives or laws. Let's just admit that, when we seek political solutions to the world's problems, it's because we've given up on changing the world by sharing the Gospel. Instead, we just want to pass laws to force people who are not Christians to act like we do so we'll feel more comfortable in this society.

No political agenda, party, system, or politician will ever bring our nation any closer to the image of God. Only Jesus can do that.

NO POLITICAL AGENDA, PARTY, SYSTEM, OR POLITICIAN WILL EVER BRING OUR NATION ANY CLOSER TO THE IMAGE OF GOD. ONLY JESUS CAN DO THAT.

Our core problems, as a human race, are spiritual in nature. The only solution is spiritual. Jesus is our answer. He is the only answer. No other additives or preservatives are required.

In fact, to the degree that we allow ourselves to be corrupted by politics and blinded by nationalism and patriotism, we play into the tactics of the enemy. As C.S. Lewis so expertly noted in *The Screwtape Letters*, the demonic strategy to manipulate us is exactly this:

> "Let him begin by treating patriotism…as a part of his religion. Then let him, under the influence of partisan spirit, come to regard it as the most important part. Then quietly and gradually nurse him on to the stage at which the religion becomes merely a part of the 'cause,' in which Christianity is valued chiefly because of the excellent arguments it can produce…once you have made the world an end, and faith a means, you have almost won your man, and it makes very little difference what kind of worldly end he is pursuing"[5]

The more we surrender ourselves to the Enemy's tactics by embracing politics and nationalism, the less effective we will be in our mission as ambassadors of Christ.

The primary function of the Church is to facilitate spiritual transformation, one person at a time. The primary function of the State is to facilitate an ordered society.

Much like Simon the Sorcerer in the book of Acts, who offered money to buy power from the apostles, the Government would love nothing more than to have the power to transform the hearts and minds of people. But unlike the apostles, today's Christians are only too willing to sell out to the State in exchange for power, influence, and tax exemption.

The irony is, we in the Church have been bamboozled to accept the lie that the State has the greater power. We believe that Christ's ability to transform hearts and minds is weaker than the power of the State to pass laws and enforce them with intimidation.

Yet, in Jesus, we have the greater power by far. We are filled with the Spirit of God and "the same power that raised Christ from the dead" is at work within us (Romans 8:11)!

Would you rather write and enforce a new law, or would you rather see God change someone's heart to reflect His own love and kindness?

According to 2 Corinthians 12:8-10, our power is displayed in weakness. Our influence is carried out in love. This means that no law can accomplish what the Gospel can.

If we doubt that this power to love, forgive, serve, and heal is truly greater than the State's power to coerce people into submission, then we have lost faith in Christ and have bowed our knees to the enemy.

And if that is the case, then may God have mercy on us all.

The truth is this: We'll never shape the world if we are not first shaped by Christ. Only the transformed can inspire transformation.

What's more, we cannot transform a culture if that culture has already transformed us.

Ed Dobson, a former spokesman for Jerry Falwell's Moral Majority during the rise of the Religious Right, has since recanted his previous position regarding the entanglement of Christianity and politics.

In the book, *Blinded By Might*, (co-authored by Cal Thomas, who also prominently helped to lead the Moral Majority), Dobson asks a profound question:

> "Did the Moral Majority really make a difference? During the height of the Moral Majority, we were taking in millions of dollars a year. We published a magazine, organized state chapters, lobbied Congress, aired a radio program, and more. Did it work? Is the moral condition of America better because of our efforts? Even a casual observation of the current moral climate suggests that despite all the time, money and energy—despite the political power—we failed. Things have not gotten better; they have gotten worse."[6]

Cal Thomas agrees that their efforts were wasted and discloses one big change that was the result of their experiences in the Moral Majority, saying:

> "What has changed is that we no longer believe that our individual or collective cultural problems can be altered exclusively, or even mainly, through the political process." [7]

> "If people who claim to follow Jesus and his kingdom get too cozy with government, it won't be the government that gets injured. It will be the church that is compromised."[8]

Later in the book, Dobson points out that:

> "Upon reflection, I think the leaders of the Religious Right have made several critical mistakes. First, they have expectations of the government that God never intended. They expect government to reflect their religious values, but it was never instituted by God to do so. It was instituted to restrain evil and promote good so that the values of God could be reflected in the lives of the people who claim to follow God. Second, [they] abandoned the greater priority of communicating the gospel for the lesser priority of sanctifying the State. The net result is that they have accomplished neither very well."[9]

In their epilogue, the two men summarize their collective experience of the fruit of entanglement of Christians in politics by saying:

> "...Perhaps it is the religious leaders who should resign from the political pulpits and devote themselves to their primary calling and what the Bible calls a Christian's 'first love': the person and work and example of Jesus Christ."[10]

> "Just because you have won an election doesn't mean you have persuaded a nation of our point of view...Consider your own experience. Have you ever brought a person to your point of view by force?"[11]

> "We don't have a shortage of leaders, but a shortage of followers of the one Leader who can transform lives and nations. We don't need to enlarge our vision, but make it smaller and more focused...Religious conservatives, no matter how well organized, can't save America. Only God can. But He will only consider doing it if God's people get out of the way and give Him room. That's the better way. It is also the only way."[12]

The question for us is: Are we willing to lay aside our lust for political power and influence in order to humble ourselves and take up the cross of Jesus?

That is the question we must answer, and for the sake of our world, our nation, and even ourselves, we must answer it correctly.

CHAPTER 6

THE SUPREMACY OF CHRIST AND THE GOSPEL

"The temptation to consider power an apt instrument for the proclamation of the gospel is the greatest temptation of all."

– HENRI J. NOUWEN

The fact that Christians turn to politics and the pursuit of influence and power to bring the gospel to the world proves without a doubt that we have failed to understand our mission, or to fully embrace the entirety of the gospel message itself.

Jesus entered this world as a subversive agent of change, intending to transform reality from the inside out.

This revolution started quietly, and largely unnoticed. Only a limited few were privy to the plan. Fewer still understood it completely.

Like a tiny bit of yeast that permeates an entire lump of dough, or like a small seed which falls to the ground and dies—only to germinate and break the surface of the soil, eventually covering the entire garden—Jesus came into this world as the smallest catalyst of all. He was a single embryo hidden inside the womb of a poor Jewish girl in Palestine.

Jesus' people were looking for a Messiah who would finally rescue them from captivity and from the oppression of the Roman Empire. They were desperate for a regime change, and most were ready to fight for it. All they needed was God's chosen liberator to lead the way.

They wanted a warrior. What they got was a baby. As Mary Emily Duba so eloquently puts it:

> "God does not come as a warrior king. God comes as a baby. God's power is hidden under the signs of vulnerability. God comes in poverty. God comes to a young woman who had no status in the community. God's glory is hidden in the ugliness of our lives. In places of violence, in places of suffering, God is there, hidden among us. This is the theology of the cross. That in the horror of the cross, in the violence, in the ugliness, and the weakness of a man stripped and beaten and hung to die there is something more powerful at work. Hidden under these signs of weakness is the glory of God."[1]

OUR QUEST FOR POWER AND INFLUENCE RUNS DIRECTLY AGAINST THE EXAMPLE AND MESSAGE OF JESUS.

Paul tells us that when God was ready to set us free and transform the world, the first thing He did was to set aside all of His power and glory:

> "In your relationships with one another, have the same mindset as Christ Jesus: Who, being in very nature God, did not consider equality with God something to be used to his own advantage; rather, *he made himself nothing by taking the very nature of a servant, being made in human likeness. And being found in appearance as a man, he humbled himself by becoming obedient to death*—even death on a cross!" (Philippians 2:5-8).

Our quest for power and influence runs directly against the example and message of Jesus. He was offered political power by Satan in the desert and He refused it.

Instead, Jesus showed us how to overcome the enemy and the world by embracing the power of weakness. It's counterintuitive to us, and it seems foolish at first—something that we're told is a normal reaction for those who do not see the Kingdom:

> "For the preaching of the cross is to them that perish foolishness; but unto us which are saved it is the power of God" (1 Corinthians 1:18).
>
> "But we preach Christ crucified, unto the Jews a stumbling block, and unto the Greeks foolishness; But unto them which are called, both Jews and Greeks, Christ the power of God, and the wisdom of God. Because the foolishness of God is wiser than men; and the weakness of God is stronger than men" (1 Corinthians 1:23-25).
>
> "But God hath chosen the foolish things of the world to confound the wise; and God hath chosen the weak things of the world to confound the things which are mighty…" (1 Corinthians 1:27).

But if we have seen the Kingdom of God, then we understand what's really going on. We realize that, for thousands of years, men and women have been responding to violence with more violence. They've been repaying evil with more evil, endlessly repeating the same mistakes over and over again.

You may have heard that the definition of insanity is doing the same things over and over again, expecting a different result. For centuries, mankind has continued in the delusion that we can make the world a better place if we could just kill enough "bad" people, or if we could just elect enough "good" leaders to rule over us. The record clearly shows us that these have never proven true. We cannot kill our way to peace, nor can we vote our way to paradise.

Jesus came to restore sanity to mankind. He showed us another way to live and a better way to be human beings.

When the Apostle Paul discovered this, he rejoiced. His epiphany came after praying for God to remove a thorn in his flesh. When God responded by saying, "My grace is sufficient for you, for *my power is made perfect in weakness*" (2 Corinthians 12:9), Paul realized what God was trying to teach him and said:

> "I will boast all the more gladly about my weaknesses, *so that Christ's power may rest on me*. That is why, for Christ's sake, *I delight in weaknesses, in insults, in hardships, in persecutions, in difficulties. For when I am weak, then I am strong*" (2 Corinthians 12:10).

Many Christians today have completely ignored, or forgotten, the simple power of weakness. The sword of Constantine is still more alluring and compelling as an instrument of change. Yet Jesus, our Lord, is quite clear that those who live by the sword will also die by the sword. Our only hope is to lay down our sword and take up our cross as Jesus commanded us. This is the only method of transformation that God has ordained and the only hope for any of us as people.

If only those who are called by His name could awaken to His voice. If only we could follow His example and not only call Him our "Lord," but actually do what He says.

G.K. Chesterton once said, "It's not that Christianity has been tried and found wanting; it's that it has been found difficult and left untried."[2]

The great irony of our blindness to the plan that Jesus has given us is that His plan is infinitely more powerful than any man-made weapon or political force.

The demonic and worldly empires are powerless to stop the power of weakness. How could anyone ever defeat an opponent who only grows stronger the weaker they become? How can anyone ever stop someone who has already died in advance? How can all the darkness in the universe overwhelm a single flame? The answer, of course, is that these things are impossible.

Yet, even though we have been handed a weapon of infinite power, we still want to rely on meager tools such as guns, bombs, and politics—tools which have never brought us anything but misery, bloodshed, despair, and frustration.

Our Father has given us an astounding gift: the power to be transformed by His love into people who are like His Son, and to become "new creatures" who have a new nature and a new heart.

We have also been offered an amazing opportunity and privilege to collaborate with Him in the ongoing transformation of the entire human race, one person at a time.

This pure love is very much like spiritual uranium. It not only has the power to transform us with prolonged contact, but it can also create an explosion of change that has the potential to transform every human life on this planet *if* we know how to use it properly.

I've been captivated lately by the image of the love of Christ as an awesome, unlimited power that has been handed down to us by the Creator of the universe.

Much like handing a toddler a nuclear warhead capable of transforming the landscape in the blink of an eye, Jesus has entrusted every one of us with the greatest force in the universe: agape love. Agape love is a love which has the power not to destroy a city, but to transform and renew all humanity from within.

If you have experienced the inexpressible power of God's love, you know what I'm talking about. It disarms you. It changes you from within. It fills your heart with unspeakable joy, impossible hope, and complete faith that the impossible is not only possible, but is also extremely likely.

You and I, as disciples of Jesus, have been handed the most astounding force of change ever devised: God's love. We have been changed by it ourselves; and the more we are exposed to it, the more we are changed daily into new creatures with new minds and new hearts. This love within us has the power to change the world. In fact, it is intended to do so. It was designed by the One who spoke the universe into existence to do just that.

This love of Christ has the power to transform the hearts, renew the minds, and restore the souls of every person with whom we come into contact. No matter who they are—atheists, rapists, murderers, drug addicts, prostitutes, LGBTs, Muslims, Baptists, Democrats, Republicans, Nazis, ISIS followers, terrorists, lawyers, professors, and so on.

Truthfully, no one is immune to the power of God's love. Some may resist it. Some may deny it. They may run from it in fear. But the power of the love of Christ to soften the heart, renew the mind, and transform the soul is irresistible.

We are living proof. The more we are exposed to this love, the more we are changed. The more we are changed, the more others around us experience that love and the cycle continues.

If you wield a force as powerful as agape love, what would you want with a gun, a knife, or a political party? These weapons are not capable of ushering in the Kingdom of God. They are only designed to end life or to control people through fear and manipulation. Our weapons are of an other-worldly design:

> "The weapons we fight with are not the weapons of the world. On the contrary, they have divine power to demolish strongholds" (2 Corinthians 10:4).

Do you believe this? Do you really believe that Jesus has entrusted us with a weapon that is mighty beyond belief? Do you honestly believe that it has the power to demolish strongholds and turn murderers into ministers, abusers into healers, terrorists into ambassadors of peace, and even persecutors of the Church into apostles of Christ?

If so, then put that faith into action. Place your hope—all of it—in the power of Christ, His love, and His Kingdom. Abandon the weapons of this world. Lay them aside and take up your cross to follow Jesus into a revolution of transformation that begins with you and ends with the whole world made new.

If only we could simply take hold of that volatile, dangerous power of love today—if we could immerse ourselves in it—if it could permeate our being, then it might just transform each of us into a living beacon of His audacious, awesome, astounding love.

Perhaps this concept is difficult for us to imagine because we so seldom see it put into practice. However, just because this is rare doesn't mean it is impossible.

ABANDON THE WEAPONS OF THIS WORLD. LAY THEM ASIDE AND TAKE UP YOUR CROSS TO FOLLOW JESUS INTO A REVOLUTION OF TRANSFORMATION THAT BEGINS WITH YOU AND ENDS WITH THE WHOLE WORLD MADE NEW.

I can remember when our oldest son, Dylan, was in first grade. He came home one day and told us about a boy in his class who was choking and kicking him at recess.

At first, I was enraged. I even considered putting my son in a karate class. Instead, my wife and I realized that we had an opportunity to put the words of Jesus into practice and to teach our son how to do the same.

So, before bedtime each night, we prayed together for this other boy. We talked about what he must be going through at home to treat others so violently. We prayed for his parents, and for his brothers and sisters. We asked Jesus to change this boy's heart.

Now, in a practical sense, we also talked to Dylan about how he should avoid being alone with this boy at recess. We encouraged him to go to his teachers if he saw this boy coming after him, or other kids, again.

Nothing seemed to change at first. However, a few weeks later, my son had a birthday party. He invited every kid in his class, including this boy who had bullied him.

During the party, this boy was included in every game. He was treated as one of my son's friends. My son, and our family, gave him the clear message: We don't hate you. We really love you.

After the party, that child no longer bullied Dylan at recess. The love my son had shown him really did transform him. It touched his heart and changed his behavior. It also changed us and the way we responded to others who wanted to harm us.

Does this surprise you? It really shouldn't. Jesus gave us another way to respond:

> "If you love those who love you, what credit is that to you? Even 'sinners' love those who love them. And if you do good to those who are good to you, what credit is that to you? Even 'sinners' do that. And if you lend to those from whom you expect repayment, what credit is that to you? Even 'sinners' lend to 'sinners,' expecting to be repaid in full. But love your enemies, do good to them, and lend to them without expecting to get anything back. Then your reward will be great, and you will be sons of the Most High, because he is kind to the ungrateful and wicked. Be merciful, just as your Father is merciful" (Luke 6:32).

Jesus contrasts the love the world has with the love that God demonstrates to us. The love of the world is nothing special. Even a murderer can love his best friend. What's special about that? But, as followers of Jesus, we are called to demonstrate the amazing, unprecedented, unexpected, over-the-top kind of love that Jesus has lavished upon us.

Why? For two reasons: First, we are called to love so that even the most evil person can experience the undeserved kindness and mercy of God. Secondly, we love because loving others teaches you and I how to die to ourselves and become more like Jesus every day.

See, the command that Jesus gives us to love our enemies is intended not only to change the hearts of sinners, but to change our own hearts as well.

We cannot love like Jesus loves on our own. The only way we can follow Jesus and obey his command to love those who are trying to harm us is if we take up our cross daily, die to ourselves, throw ourselves completely at His feet, and beg to be filled with His love for our enemies. It just won't work any other way.

As Jesus reminds us, "Apart from me, you can do nothing" (John 15:5).

In the book, *The Grace of Giving,* author Stephen Olford tells the story of a Baptist pastor during the American Revolution. The pastor, Peter Miller, lived in Ephrata, Pennsylvania, and one of his dearest friends was General George Washington. (Maybe you've heard of him?)

In the town of Ephrata there also lived a spiteful trouble-maker named Michael Wittman who did all he could to oppose and humiliate Mr. Miller.

One day, Michael Wittman was arrested for treason and sentenced to death. When he heard the news, Peter Miller set out to Philadelphia to plead for the life of his enemy.

After walking seventy miles—on foot—Miller petitioned his friend, General Washington, to spare Wittman's life.

"No, Peter," General Washington said. "I cannot grant you the life of your friend."

"My friend?" exclaimed the old preacher. "He's not my friend. In fact, he is the bitterest enemy I have."

"What?" cried Washington. "You've walked seventy miles to save the life of an enemy? That puts the matter in different light. I'll grant your pardon."

And he did.

That day, Peter Miller and Michael Wittman walked back home to Ephrata together. When they arrived home, they were no longer enemies. They were friends.

Peter Miller had a different perspective when it came to resolving conflict. He looked for opportunities to love others the way Jesus does. You and I are expected to do the same.

> "Do not repay evil with evil or insult with insult, but with blessing, because *to this you were called* so that you may inherit a blessing" (1 Peter 3:9).

CHRIST'S PLAN INVOLVES PREEMPTIVE LOVE AND PROACTIVE AGAPE.

As followers of Jesus, you and I are to be living examples of the redemptive, transformative power of undeserved kindness and love.

See, our Lord Jesus has a plan to overcome the world. But it will only work if the people who are called by His Name are willing to put it into action. That plan is to love others unconditionally like He loves them.

Scoffers might respond by asking how a strategy like this can stop terrorism or mass shootings. It's a valid question; but we have to understand that once a person has decided in their heart to kill others, there's not much we can do about it. Christ's plan is a preemptive and proactive one. It's designed to transform people from potential killers into Christians so that they don't want to harm anyone else.

In other words, the way we stop mass murderers and terrorists is to show them the love of Christ before they pick up their weapons, not after. Christ's plan involves preemptive love and proactive agape.

Always remember that following Jesus may get you in trouble. It may even get you killed. This is why Jesus declared that no one could start following Him without first laying down their life, denying themselves, and taking up their own cross daily.

The plan is simple: Jesus wants to change the world with love. We are His ambassadors. He has given us the ministry of reconciliation. He has called us to be peacemakers. He has commanded us to be known for our love—love that even extends to the enemy holding a high-powered rifle.

If we are successful, fewer people will want to pick up a weapon to kill anyone else because Jesus will have transformed their hearts. If we fail, we might be "counted as sheep to be slaughtered" (see Romans 8:36).

We have to abandon the myth that we can make the world a better place by just killing enough people. We have to admit that killing to protect others falls under the same category as "loving those who love you in return."

Instead, Jesus calls us to something greater: something audacious and extraordinary. He calls us to love dangerously; to lay down our lives so that others may have the opportunity to know the transformative love of Christ.

This mission is not for the faint of heart. We must count the cost. We must decide in advance that our lives are already lost for the sake of Jesus and His Kingdom.

Quite often, Christians who favor the use of violence will say that we should protect the innocent. The assumption being that protecting the innocent must involve the use of force. But that is not necessarily so.

Yes, it is true that 1 Corinthians 13:6 tells us that "Love always protects," but let's ask a few questions first:

Do we ever see Jesus protecting the innocent with violence?

Does Jesus ever command us to protect the safety of others?

Do we ever see the Apostles, or any of the earliest Christians, protecting one another from danger or death?

Surprisingly, we do not. What, then, does Paul mean when he says that "Love always protects?"

I think it depends on what you mean by "protect." We can safely say that whatever Paul means here, he does not intend to justify the use of violence. But he also doesn't mean "do nothing while people get brutalized" either.

Believe it or not, there is a middle ground between doing nothing and the use of deadly force.

For those who seek to follow Jesus and to embody the practice of agape love, protection looks like stepping in front of the bullet, or inserting your body between the victim and the attacker. It means sacrificing yourself to save someone else.

I heard someone tell a personal story once that illustrated this kind of love perfectly.

Several years ago, my friend (we'll call him Joe), was visiting India. As a young Christian, he wanted to save the world, and he was naïve enough to think he could bring the Kingdom all by himself.

One day he was walking the streets of Delhi and he came upon a circle of policemen beating an old man with their clubs.

In a surreal moment, they stopped and turned slowly to look at him as he approached. He was the only white man on the street. They waited to see what he would say, what he would do. Even the old man, trembling and bleeding there on the street, looked up at him and waited to see what he would do.

In a moment of shameful indecision and impotence my friend, not knowing what else he could do, just kept on walking, and as he walked away he heard the beating continue.

When he got back to his room he wept and cried out to God to forgive him for his embarrassing failure to act.

About five years later, this same friend found himself living in the home of a poor family in Santa Ana, California, as a guest.

He wasn't there to change the world. He now simply wanted to learn first-hand about the struggles people endured on a daily basis. He wanted to learn how to serve others, and to love as Jesus loved.

One day he heard shouting outside on the street. He looked out the window and saw the teenage boy from the family he was staying with being beaten by a local gang.

Immediately, he ran outside and pushed his way through the circle. When he saw this boy laying on the ground, my friend did not hesitate; he quickly covered the boy with his own body and took those kicks and punches himself. After a moment, everything stopped. The gang leader shouted at him to get out of the way. He refused. "You're loco," they told him. But he didn't move, so they eventually left.

Afterwards, my friend said he started thinking about why he had done that. The Lord showed him. "Your love compelled you," he heard the Spirit whisper, and then his mind flashed back to that memory, years ago in India, when he had seen that old man being beaten and had done nothing.

WE WILL PROTECT OTHERS, NOT WITH VIOLENCE, BUT WITH SACRIFICIAL DEVOTION.

He understood, at last, what the difference was. It was love. He didn't need to think about what to do when his heart was filled with love for his friend.

As our hearts are filled more and more with the love of Christ, we also will respond as His love compels us. We will, like Jesus, lay down our lives for one another.

We will protect others, not with violence, but with sacrificial devotion.

"Greater love has no man than this: to lay down his life for a friend" (John 15:13)

CHAPTER 7

THE CONSPIRACY OF ENTANGLEMENT

"To be a Christian, one must pledge their allegiance to Christ and his Kingdom. At that point, all other prior allegiances—including allegiance to one's birth nation—immediately become null and void."

– BENJAMIN L. COREY

As we've already seen, the Church first became entangled with Empire and enamored with politics and all that goes with it—nationalism, patriotism, militarism, and violence—during the reign of the Emperor Constantine.

But the history of entanglement repeats itself many times throughout history.

Christians in the first three hundred years of the faith were not tempted to become entangled with politics or to advance the Gospel by passing laws. Some say it's because the Roman Empire was so pagan and evil that no Christian would want to participate in it. Truly, however, it was no more evil than any other worldly empire. Historically, there were many Roman soldiers and political officials who actually did convert to the faith.

In fact, this happened often enough that several early Christian teachers created a policy for how to respond to this trend.

As Hippolytus of Rome said:

> "A soldier of the civil authority must be taught not to kill men and to refuse to do so if he is commanded, and to refuse to take an oath. If he is unwilling to comply, he must be rejected for baptism. A military commander or civic magistrate must resign or be rejected. If a believer seeks to become a soldier, he must be rejected, for he has despised God."[1]

And as we have already seen, Origen made it clear that:

> "It is not for the purpose of escaping public duties that Christians decline public offices, but so that they may reserve themselves for a more divine and more necessary service in the Church of God—the salvation of men. And this service is at once necessary and right."

So, the early church certainly had the opportunity to take full advantage of a growing number of political converts in positions of power throughout the Roman Empire. Why not capitalize on that? Why not infiltrate the military command and turn the sword away from the throats of their martyred brothers and sisters?

Why? Because they saw clearly that political entanglement was a snare and a distraction from their main mission. Furthermore, they were unwavering in their devotion to Jesus and to His Kingdom. They stayed the course. They kept the faith.

If the early Christians understood who they were and what their mission was so clearly, why do so many believers today find it impossible to imagine following Jesus apart from political affiliation?

As my friend Ross Rohde has pointed out, when the Religious Right aligned itself with the Republican party to help elect Ronald Reagan, that foolish compromise started a snowball effect that we are still suffering from today. Now, millions of American Christians can no longer imagine Christianity apart from conservative Republicanism.

As Ross put it:

> "In my opinion the Republican party has prostituted the American Evangelical church. They (now) own us and our thinking. We end up holding values that are counter to the values of Jesus because they've got us thinking along their paradigms rather than us evaluating everything according to the stated values of Jesus and the example of His life."[2]

Ross goes on to say that the American Church has become ensnared in much the same way that a pimp grooms a new prostitute—seeking the girl who is pretty, but not the center of attention. By manipulating her need to be noticed and valued, the pimp can exploit her and get her to believe that if she just keeps doing what the pimp asks her to do, "one day" she will realize her dreams.

NOW, MILLIONS OF AMERICAN CHRISTIANS CAN NO LONGER IMAGINE CHRISTIANITY APART FROM CONSERVATIVE REPUBLICANISM.

But it's all a lie.

For more than 40 years now, the Republican Party has been promising American Christians that they will overturn Roe v. Wade and outlaw abortion again. We've had two terms of Reagan, one term of George Bush, two terms of George W. Bush, *and* a majority Republican Congress during many of those years—and what have they done?

Not much.

The truth is, the abortion issue is a "shiny red button" that the Republican Party loves to hold out to us as a way to manipulate us to vote for their candidate. But once that person is elected the issue of abortion is never a priority for that politician.

Here's why: The "shiny red button" works as it was designed to work. It makes us vote for them. That's all it is supposed to do.

When I was much younger, my Dad told me something that has always stayed with me. He said that there was no money in finding a cure for cancer, for muscular dystrophy, or for many of the other diseases in our world today. "There's only money in *looking* for a cure," he said. And he is right. There are billions of dollars raised every year for research, and billions more in the sale of medicines which treat the symptoms of these diseases. Why would anyone be so foolish as to cure the disease when the end result would be to dry up the endless stream of revenues?

It's no different with the abortion issue. The "shiny red button" works every time they hold it out to us. The light blinks. We vote. They win. The button goes back into the box until the next election. If they ever solve the problem and outlaw abortion, they will have no way to stir up the votes for their candidates.

Simply put, the abortion issue is nothing more than a means to manipulate the evangelical Christians in America to vote for Republican candidates.

The Christian leaders who formed the Moral Majority learned this lesson the hard way. They got cozy with Ronald Reagan and registered thousands of Christians to vote Republican on the promise that he was "on our side" and would give us legitimacy, restore our respect among the culture, and take a stand for "Christian values." But none of that never happened.

In fact, what did happen was that Reagan, after only one month into his Presidency, appointed Sandra Day O'Connor to the Supreme Court. Was she a pro-life Conservative who would make good on his promise to overturn Roe v. Wade? Hardly. In fact, she has been the pro-choice swing vote in virtually every abortion-related case before the Supreme Court.

Does this surprise you? There's more. The fact is that the majority of Supreme Court Justices who ruled in the Roe v. Wade case were Conservative appointees.

The Southern Baptist Convention's former president, W. A. Criswell, even published a response after the ruling where he said:

> "I have always felt that it was only after a child was born and had a life separate from its mother that it became an individual person ... and it has always, therefore, seemed to me that what is best for the mother and for the future should be allowed."[3]

And W. Barry Garrett of the *Baptist Press* said, "Religious liberty, human equality and justice are advanced by the Supreme Court abortion decision…"[4]

And, shockingly, in 1971, delegates to the Southern Baptist Convention in St. Louis, Missouri, passed a resolution encouraging Southern Baptists to, "work for legislation that will allow the possibility of abortion under such conditions as rape, incest, clear evidence of severe fetal deformity, and carefully ascertained evidence of the likelihood of damage to the emotional, mental, and physical health of the mother."[5]

They reaffirmed this resolution the year after the Roe v. Wade ruling, and again in 1976.[6]

Clearly, the issue of abortion was not a high-priority one for Religious Conservatives in the early 70s. It only became an issue when it conveniently served as the catalyst for Republicans to win votes and for evangelical Christians to become politically influential.

Falwell himself was never moved by abortion and often spoke out against Christians becoming entangled by politics as he did in a sermon back in 1965 called "Of Ministers and Marchers" where he argued that the duty of ministers was simply to preach the gospel of Jesus Christ, not to become involved in Civil

Rights reforms, and not to become involved in anti-communism or anything else.

According to Frank Schaeffer, the son of Francis Schaeffer, his father was the first one to speak up:

> "Dad is the one who talked Jerry Falwell personally into taking a stand on abortion. Before that, Jerry Falwell said, "That's a Catholic issue. It's nothing to do with us. Why would I want to take a stand on that? I'm just a preacher. I want to talk about the gospel."[7]

With the help of Francis Schaeffer and C. Everett Koop, however, Falwell and others became persuaded to rally Christians in America to embrace political activism as a means to overturn Roe v. Wade, and, at the same time, to help elect Ronald Reagan into office.

As Frank Schaeffer remembers:

> "Dad was very persuasive, and the word began to spread. But then we also made some converts to our cause who were in positions of influence—for instance, Congressman Jack Kemp, who then invited us back to the Republican Club in an evening hosted by him and Bob Dole. And then soon after that, Dad met with Ronald Reagan and talked about this. They began to see it as a way to win elections. We began to see winning elections as a way to make our country a better moral place."[8]

Unfortunately, the only thing they accomplished was electing Ronald Reagan into office. Once he was in the White House, the promises made were not kept.

As Reverend Richard Cizik remarked:

> "Ronald Reagan knew how to please evangelicals without giving them anything in return. Major constitutional amendments went nowhere. And the White House gave lip service to these. I know. I heard the lip service all the time. But…they wouldn't spend the president's capital to go to Capitol Hill and lobby legislators on behalf of these ideas, not really."[9]

And Ed Dobson concurs, asking, "What did Reagan do for us in eight years of office? He gave us credibility, and he ultimately did nothing in terms of our long-term agendas."[10]

As Cal Thomas, one of the founding members of the Moral Majority said:

> "If any political movement should have been able to change the country by implementing its agenda, it was the Moral Majority. We had the nation's attention. We were mobilizing the nation's largest demographic unit...and we had a President in the White House friendly to our objectives. For six years we also had a Republican-controlled Senate.
>
> Our people were welcome in the White House, which some had never dreamed of visiting other than on the public tour. We were advancing. Liberalism was retreating. It was just a matter of time before our nation would be restored to what we wanted it to be. Those who doubted or questioned our power were dismissed. Those who warned of danger ahead were ignored, ridiculed or condemned.
>
> That was twenty years ago, and today very little that we set out to do has gotten done. In fact, the moral landscape of America has become worse."[11]

As sobering as this may be, it's only a more recent example of how the Christian Church in America became entangled with politics. It's not where the pimping of American Christianity really began.

As Princeton historian Kevin Kruse details in his book, *One Nation Under God: How Corporate America Invented Christian America,* our country's religious prostitution really began in the 1950s.

In his book, Kruse explains how business leaders plotted to link Christianity, Republican politics, and libertarian economics tightly together. Why? To help drive a wave of public piety and create a feeling of solidarity between Christians and corporations who might both see "Big Government" as a common enemy.

This is where our national motto, "In God We Trust" (1956), and the new line in the Pledge of Allegiance, "One nation under God" (1954) was added.

And the goal was simple: to entangle Christianity with Republican politics in order to benefit big business. As Kruse explains:

> "The reason they [corporations] start making this argument about freedom under God is that it's a much more effective way to push back against the regulatory state and the labor unions. It's no longer businessmen making the case for businesses. It's ministers."[12]

And why Christian ministers? Because they were better at propaganda. "They're very effective at making this argument that a state that restricts capitalism will inevitably restrict Christianity," says Kruse. "They link economic restrictions with religious restrictions. It requires a bit of a leap of faith, but it's one that they effectively sell."

Other historians agree, including Kim Phillips-Fein whose book, *Invisible Hands,* also documents this unholy alliance between 1950s corporations and the Christian Church.

AND THE GOAL WAS SIMPLE: TO ENTANGLE CHRISTIANITY WITH REPUBLICAN POLITICS IN ORDER TO BENEFIT BIG BUSINESS.

Both Phillips-Fein and Kruse credit a pastor by the name of Reverend Fifield—whose large Los Angeles congregation was made up mostly of millionaires—as one of the most effective ministers in the capitalistic Christian movement. "Fifield disregards all of Christ's warnings about the dangers of wealth," says Kruse. "He completely disregards the injunction to look out for one another. To love your neighbor, to be your brother's keeper. He discards all of those messages. It becomes a faith of individualism."

In order to make it all work, the teachings of Jesus had to be downplayed. The Sermon on the Mount needed to be mothballed in favor of more sermons about individual faith, civic duty, and paying taxes. Christianity began to slowly mirror the ideals of capitalism, and soon enough Jesus was re-branded as the poster boy for the American Dream.

Another minister, James Ingebretsen, President of a group known as Spiritual Mobilization (itself created by Reverend Fifield to further this same cause) also admitted: "Fighting the forces that wanted to abolish the free enterprise system was my mission, not promoting Christ."[13]

This well-funded crusade to entangle the Christian faith with Republican conservatism gained momentum in the 1970s and 1980s as evangelical leaders like Pat Robertson and Jerry Falwell took the wheel. As Phillips-Fein notes in her book, one of the leading fund raisers for this movement, Richard Viguerie, affirmed that "the next real major area of growth for the conservative ideology and philosophy is among evangelical people."

And what was the result? As Kruse explains, "[this movement] had been launched to roll back the New Deal and instead it helps inspire a new sort of religious nationalism."

My question for you is, "Did it work?"

Have you bought their propaganda? Is your faith now entangled with conservative Republican values? Are you, even now, still unable to separate your faith in Jesus from your political ideology?

I must confess that I was a victim of this propaganda. I was raised in a Republican home. I voted in every election since I was legally able to vote and I always voted "straight ticket" Republican.

I listened to Rush Limbaugh. I read his books. I watched the Republican National Convention every election year on television.

I cheered for my Republican President, and I griped and complained about those liberal Democrats who were ruining our nation and threatening to bring down the wrath of God upon us.

But it was—and it is—all a lie.

It's manipulation. Pure and simple.

We are all the victims of a well-funded, decades-long campaign to twist our faith into an easy-to-control voting block.

This is why it is so imperative for us to open our eyes, throw off the chains and return to Jesus—and Jesus alone—as our Lord and King.

You've no doubt heard Christian pastors and teachers warn you that voting for a pro-choice candidate makes you guilty of murder. I recently heard this argument on a Christian radio show:

> "If you vote for a candidate who is going to continue to promote murder, then are you not an accessory to murder? Even if your vote alone wouldn't put them into office—because many people will obviously vote—but if you know for a fact that this person is going to promote murder [abortion], then you're putting that person in a position to kill millions of babies every year. So, I would think voting for a candidate who you know is going to promote the murder of babies, would make you, also, a promoter of the murder of babies. How could it not be? Any person you put into office, knowing what their policies are, you are in a sense, stamping your approval on those policies."[14]

If this is true, then those who vote for a pro-war candidate are also guilty of bloodshed when innocent women and children are bombed in foreign lands. I can't think of a better reason why Christians should not vote at all. If we inherit the bloodguilt of the Presidents we vote for, then no President is innocent because our nation has been at war somewhere in the world for 214 years out of the last 235 years.[15]

That's a lot of bloodshed.

So, I encourage you to read these verses with new eyes:

> "Let us throw off everything that hinders and the sin that so *easily entangles.* And let us run with perseverance the race marked out for us" (Hebrews 12:1).

> "No one serving as a soldier *gets entangled in civilian affairs,* but rather tries to please his commanding officer" (2 Timothy 2:4).

> "But whatever were gains to me I now consider loss for the sake of Christ … *I consider them garbage, that I may gain Christ* and be found in him" (Philippians 3:7-9).

Maybe it's time for us to take out our garbage. Maybe it's time for us to finally and completely untangle ourselves from anything and everything that hinders us from following Jesus.

Let's be clear. The answer to all of this is not to join the Democratic Party, the Libertarian Party, or even to create our own political party. No, the answer is to abandon politics completely, to re-focus our eyes on Jesus, and to place our faith in His plan to change the world.

THE ANSWER TO ALL OF THIS IS NOT TO JOIN THE DEMOCRATIC PARTY, THE LIBERTARIAN PARTY, OR EVEN TO CREATE OUR OWN POLITICAL PARTY. NO, THE ANSWER IS TO ABANDON POLITICS COMPLETELY, TO RE-FOCUS OUR EYES ON JESUS, AND TO PLACE OUR FAITH IN HIS PLAN TO CHANGE THE WORLD.

The American Church must return to Her Bridegroom. She must remember Her first love.

Here's an idea: Sit down tonight with your Bible. Open up to the Gospel of Matthew. Find the Sermon on the Mount and read it slowly. As you do, listen to Jesus with a new heart.

While you read, I would like to challenge you to crucify your nationalism; to crucify your political affiliation; and to put to death anything that exalts itself against the Lordship of Jesus.

I challenge you to follow Jesus totally untangled from this world.

> "They promise them freedom, while they themselves are slaves of depravity—for 'people are slaves to whatever has mastered them.' If they have escaped the corruption of the world by knowing our Lord and Savior Jesus Christ *and are again entangled in it and are overcome,* they are worse off at the end than they were at the beginning" (2 Peter 2:19-20).

You may not realize it, but there was a very successful pro-life movement that started in the 1860s. At that time, abortion was so commonplace that advertisements for abortions ran in the newspapers. The abortion rate, adjusting for per capita statistics, was as large as what America endured in the post-Roe v. Wade era.

In the book, *Abortion in America*, by James C. Mohr, this time between 1840 and 1880 is referred to as "The Great Upsurge of Abortion." Estimates are that at least 20 percent of pregnancies were ending in induced abortion during that time in history.

Another book, *The Great Crime of the Nineteenth Century*, by Edmund Hale, claimed two-thirds of pregnancies during the mid-to-late 1800s ended in induced abortions.

It was a dark time.

However, by 1910, that abortion rate had been cut in half by a movement of Christians who provided women with positive alternatives to abortion. They focused on helping young, pregnant women in poor communities—including prostitutes—to carry their children full-term. After delivery, they either helped each young mother find adoptive parents for her child, or they stood by her to help her keep her child.

Those Christians truly focused on serving women in trouble. They committed themselves to providing practical alternatives to abortion. They sought to transform society from within—one person at a time—rather than by laws alone.

Based on this historical example, if our passion is to end abortion in our nation, the best way to do so is to circumvent political processes (which, to date, have not proven very effective), and to love our neighbor as Jesus commanded.

If we commit ourselves to sharing the love of Christ with those around us, we might just discover that Jesus was right all along about how to change our world for the better.

CHAPTER 8

HOW AMERICAN EMPIRE WORKS[1]

"The weakness of so many modern Christians is that they feel too much at home in the world."

– A.W. TOZER

Who benefits from poverty? The rich do. In other words, the only way a very few people can maintain a great amount of wealth is for a very large group of people to be kept in poverty.

So, exploitation is a necessity to perpetuate the American dream.

How do they do it? By virtually enslaving Third World countries through billions of dollars of debt which we know they can never repay.

But first let's answer the obvious question: How can we call America an empire if it doesn't have an emperor?

Just because there is not one person ruling America doesn't mean it does not qualify as an empire. It has simply evolved into a different kind of empire, where corporations are in control of the government and only a handful of people who run those corporations are in power.

In many cases, those who run the corporations and those who run the government are the same people who rotate in and out of the two seats of power (see Appendix). Some refer to this growing phenomenon as "Revolving Door Politics" where legislators move freely between roles as public servants and executive positions of power at large banks, law firms, military contractors, lobbyist agencies and other companies where they typically earn millions of dollars. One study conducted in 2011 found that nearly 5,400 former congressional staffers and 400 former U.S. lawmakers left Capitol Hill to become federal lobbyists over a 10 year period.[2] So, it really doesn't matter whether or not there is a Republican or a Democrat in the White House or if one party has a majority in Congress. Other than a few minor details, there are no significant differences between one or the other. Mainly because both parties are largely controlled by the same powerful corporations.

IN MANY CASES, THOSE WHO RUN THE CORPORATIONS AND THOSE WHO RUN THE GOVERNMENT ARE THE SAME PEOPLE WHO ROTATE IN AND OUT OF THE TWO SEATS OF POWER.

From the standpoint of expanding the American Empire, which happens under both regimes, the corporations remain in power. One year a Senator or Congressman may leave office to become CEO of a large corporation, or a CEO might be appointed to Secretary of Agriculture, Commerce, Defense, etc. Either way, whether they are in the CEO's chair or in the government office, their power and influence is undeniable and irresistible. Examples of this famously include former Vice President Dick Cheney who also served as Chairman and CEO of Halliburton, but there are many, many other examples of this revolving door between government office and the private sector.

From a historical perspective, empires have had an interesting evolution. For several thousand years, empires throughout history not only expanded their power, but also increased civilization. The Spanish, Portuguese, French, English, and many others were competing to grow their world-wide influence and establish greater control over other nations. This was accomplished mostly through warfare, and often through colonization as well. The goal was very simple: Take valuable resources from smaller, weaker nations and grow your own nation's wealth in the process. America itself is the by-product of that old style of empire-building by the English. If England had not established a colony in the Americas, there would never have been an opportunity for those colonists to rebel against their King to establish the United States of America.

That system of empire-building was out in the open and everyone understood that when one nation invaded another or when people were abducted to serve as slaves in another nation, this was part of what it meant to live in a world ruled by empire.

Today, the process of empire-building is more subtle, and is largely hidden from view. Here's how it began to shift:

- Around the time of World War II, the concepts of imperialism and colonialism began to fall out of fashion. No one wanted to be compared to Nazi Germany, so being an empire and expanding global power had to take on a different form.

- It all started with the creation of the World Bank, and eventually the International Monetary Fund (IMF) and the United Nations. The idea was to create a "new world order."

- America, in possession of atomic energy and nuclear weapons, took the seat of power in the world. The new enemy was communism. The new focus was on convincing other nations to align themselves with American capitalism, and not with their rivals the communists (Soviet Russia and China).

- American corporations began to strengthen their partnership with the World Bank and with the IMF. They launched a very pervasive propaganda campaign to convince the American public that what's good for American business is good for America, and the World.

- Soon, the benefits and virtues of greed began to be taught in our business schools. Eventually it was an almost unquestioned fact that increasing wealth for American businesses was the de-facto goal of our nation, and no one questioned how that might be accomplished.

- Most people still believed that imperialism and colonialism were a bad idea. They knew they didn't want to be like Hitler, like the *conquistadores*, or like the British Empire and roll into weaker nations with brute force. So, they redefined their methods and found news ways to expand the American empire.

The most startling example of this new paradigm came when America sought to disrupt the Iranian government after their democratically-elected leader started to nationalize their oil companies. He wanted to keep Iranian oil for Iran. This threatened American oil business in the region.

To stop this, we sent in a CIA operative whose mission was simple: Restore control of Iranian oil resources to protect American corporate interests.

Kermit Roosevelt, the son of Teddy Roosevelt, was that operative, and he was surprisingly successful in deposing Iran's leader and replacing him with a dictator, the Shah of Iran. The best thing was that he did it quietly, without a war, and it only cost a few million dollars.

The pattern worked so wonderfully, it was soon adopted and proliferated—with a few minor tweaks—across the board and soon became part of the playbook for how to virtually colonize other nations without the need to actually establish a colony.

Under the old way of empire-building, the aggressor took on large amounts of responsibility. The conquering nation had to build roads, provide education and healthcare, and oversee the national economy. But under this new method, none of that was necessary. American corporations could have their way and take hold of the natural resources without taking any responsibility for the people in that nation.

It was the perfect solution because it maximized profitability and minimized responsibility.

Here's how the new system of Empire-building really works today:

- Corporations identify a nation with resources they want to control. This could be oil, coal, opium, etc.

- Next they arrange a huge loan for that country through the World Bank or another lending arm.

- That money doesn't go to the people of that nation. Instead, it goes directly to the large corporations like Halliburton, Bechtel, or other American companies, who make a fortune on large infrastructure projects in those nations.

- Those American organizations build power plants, industrial parks, ports, and other projects.

- The poorest people in that nation do not benefit from these because they are not connected to the electrical grid; they are not educated enough to work in the industrial park; etc.

- Still, those poor citizens are left holding onto the massive debt from the loan. A few of the wealthy in that nation do get rich, but only a few.

- Once the debt reaches a critical mass, corporations send in a negotiator. The negotiator convinces the leader of that nation to sell their resources to American corporations for a discount price, to pay off their debt.

- Often, they will ask for more favors—like sending troops to support American forces in other nations or voting with the US at the United Nations.

In short, Americans loan these weaker countries money, which enriches American corporations; but then the debt for that massive loan is used as leverage to exploit their national resources—which further enriches American corporations.

Over time this process has resulted in an American empire, run by American corporations, which enslaves Third World nations and enriches American billionaires.

This American empire is largely proliferated without going to war, and without even alerting the American public that it's even taking place.

But what happens when the leader of a nation refuses to play this game? Well, a bribe is offered to them, usually millions of dollars. If they still refuse? They are either assassinated or otherwise removed from power and replaced with someone who will play this game.[3]

America has done this over and over again—in Iran, in Iraq, in Guatemala, in Chile, Ecuador, and many, many other nations over the years.[4]

If they refuse the bribe—and if they cannot be taken out of power—then, and only then, do corporations use their power to bring in the US military (as we did in Iraq, for example).

If there is corruption around the globe, we might ask, "Who is doing the corrupting?" But, we may not like the answer.

Our practice of American empire-building is also what drives illegal immigration into our country. Because this process has created such horrific poverty in Third World nations, these people naturally seek out a better life in America, where there is more opportunity.

IF THERE IS CORRUPTION AROUND THE GLOBE, WE MIGHT ASK, "WHO IS DOING THE CORRUPTING?" BUT, WE MAY NOT LIKE THE ANSWER.

Now, imagine if we stopped exploiting those nations. What if we helped develop education, sanitation, healthcare and economic stability instead of stealing their national resources? They would have no reason to risk their lives to enter our country in search of a better life.

Are we really committed to ending illegal immigration? Then we should seriously consider ending our corporate stranglehold on developing nations. By making the lives of people in other nations better, we will ultimately make our own lives better.

In other words, if we bless them, we will also be blessed.

CHAPTER 9

WHY YOUR VOTE DOESN'T COUNT[1]

"When I'm looking for a leader who's going to fight ISIS and keep this nation secure, I don't want some meek and mild leader or somebody who's going to turn the other cheek. I've said I want the meanest, toughest SOB I can find to protect this nation."

– PASTOR ROBERT JEFFRESS, FIRST BAPTIST CHURCH, DALLAS[2]

Researchers at Princeton University recently looked at 20 years' worth of data to answer the question: "Does the US government represent the people?"[3]

The results were alarming: The correlation between issues that American citizens support and the likelihood of that idea being legislated was negligible. In other words, it made absolutely no difference whether the American people supported or even wanted legislation on a particular issue or not; the Government did whatever it wanted, regardless of the level of popular support for that issue.

Let that sink in: The number of voters who were for or against any idea had no impact whatsoever on whether Congress would make that idea a law or not.

To quote the actual study: "The preferences of the average American appear to have only a miniscule, near zero, statistically non-significant impact upon public policy."

Is that what you had in mind when you imagined a government "by the people, for the people and of the people"? Hardly.

But the study also revealed another alarming fact: Those who had influence—the extremely wealthy, corporations, those who could buy lobbyists to promote their interests—were much more likely to have their way in Congress.

The real injustice of this is that this same group of people—the ultra-rich and large corporations—pay little to no taxes. This means they get what they want and everyone else—the middle class and the lower class—pay for it, whether they want to or not.

"THE PREFERENCES OF THE AVERAGE AMERICAN APPEAR TO HAVE ONLY A MINISCULE, NEAR ZERO, STATISTICALLY NON-SIGNIFICANT IMPACT UPON PUBLIC POLICY."

How does this keep happening? Because it is perfectly legal to buy political influence in America.

Large corporations can use their influence to pass any laws they want—laws that benefit them and leave the average taxpayer holding the bag—by simply spending money on a lobbyist who will influence Congress to pass such a law.

For example, the average American taxpayer would never be in favor of a law that forced them to pay for mistakes made by those large corporations. Nevertheless, that doesn't matter. The American Congress doesn't care what the average American taxpayer wants. (Remember what the Princeton study revealed?)

It's perfectly legal for large corporations to hire lobbyists who will donate to the re-election campaigns of our Congressmen and Senators. It's perfectly legal for those lobbyists to offer those same Congressional leaders million-dollar jobs at their firms.

Many lobbyists even go so far as to write the bills they want Congress to pass, and to hand those bills to their representatives. The Congressmen often don't even read the entire bill before they introduce it, vote on it, and pass it into law.[4]

It doesn't matter if those Congressmen are Republican, Democrat, Independent, or Libertarian. This is how our government works, and it has been this way for a very long time.

In just the last five years, the 200 most politically-active companies in the United States spent 5.8 billion dollars to influence the government. In return, those same companies received 4.4 trillion dollars in taxpayer support.[5] If you have enough money, you can buy political influence in America, and it is perfectly legal in every way.

The only way out of this spiral is to make corruption illegal. However, to do that, you'll need a lot of money to buy lobbyists who will then have to convince Congressmen to pass a law that will take millions of dollars out of their own pockets.

Good luck with that.

CHAPTER 10

THE POWER OF FEAR

"We live in a time where the politics of fear are the most persuasive thing on the table."

– EDWARD SNOWDEN[1]

In the book, *The Jihad of Jesus*, author Dave Andrews points out something profound about how the United States military conditions young recruits to embrace a killer instinct:

- **Frame killing as protecting or saving lives:** The only way to save lives of those you love is to kill others.
- **Portray the enemy as sub-human:** It's easier to kill people if you don't identify with them or if you think of them as "evil" or as animals.
- **Demand obedience to leaders:** Men will do almost anything if they are under strong social pressure to comply.
- **Develop the capacity for collective violence:** Accentuate their fear of letting their squad down. Diffuse responsibility across the group.

- **Increase the distance between the trigger and the target:** It's easier to kill from a distance with drones, missiles, bombs, etc. Talk about firing at targets, not people. Speak of sinking ships, not of drowning sailors. Frame the violence so it is an object being destroyed, not another human being.

The book goes on to point out how these same methods are being employed by our media to socialize us towards the redemptive qualities of violence.

I believe Andrews may be on to something. Just try to find a summer blockbuster where the hero doesn't use a gun. Try to watch a TV show where violence isn't the solution to the problem.

It seems all of our heroes carry weapons. Revenge is second nature. Retribution is justice. Death is the penalty for those who dare to threaten us. Love is reserved only for those who are like us.

Sure, we can forgive a teammate, but never an enemy. Even sympathetic villains are doomed to die in the end. A fair trial isn't satisfying. Rehabilitation is a myth. Reconciliation is a joke. We want blood, and we get it. Lots of it.

This is our status quo.

How far apart are we, really, from the coliseums of Rome?

We are so out of touch with the reality of our own bloodthirst that we are oblivious to the symbolism reflecting back at us. In *The Hunger Games*, for example, we recoil at seeing a society where the poor are forced to fight to preserve a corrupt system, but we fail to see how our own poor make up the majority of our armed forces—because they cannot find employment elsewhere and a college education isn't an option apart from becoming a soldier in the United States Armed Forces.

So, while we cheer for Katniss in *The Hunger Games* as she defies her oppressive government, we would never tolerate anyone who refused to place their hand over their heart and pledge allegiance to our flag at a football game.

We are immune to the irony. We are immune to the culture of violence in which we are immersed. Even those who claim to follow the great "Prince of Peace" will threaten to beat you if you dare suggest that violence isn't something that Jesus would allow them as an essential right of expression or self-defense. (Yes, I have experienced this personally).

So much of our media today is driven by fear. Sit and watch the evening news—both local and national—and make a note of how often you hear words like "fear," "disturbing," "worry," "warning," "terror," "horror," "threat," and similar fear-based adjectives. The results will surprise you.

EVEN THOSE WHO CLAIM TO FOLLOW THE GREAT "PRINCE OF PEACE" WILL THREATEN TO BEAT YOU IF YOU DARE SUGGEST THAT VIOLENCE ISN'T SOMETHING THAT JESUS WOULD ALLOW THEM AS AN ESSENTIAL RIGHT OF EXPRESSION OR SELF-DEFENSE.

Or, maybe they won't.

The truth is, this has been going on for some time now. Author David Altheide has written several books documenting this disturbing trend, such as *Media Power, Terrorism and the Politics of Fear,* and *Creating Fear: News and the Construction of a Crisis.* All of these books document the media's purposeful use of language that incites fear and keeps people in a constant state of uncertainty and unease.

As Altheide notes:

> "Social life starts to change because of it, and we start altering our lives…We don't go out as much. Architecturally, we protect ourselves with gated communities, high walls and no windows. Public space begins to decline."[2]

Over time, as we are programmed to feel afraid for our safety, we begin to believe that the world is more violent—when crime is actually in decline.[3] We become convinced that threats to our health, safety, and way of life are everywhere; and all we can do is to lock our doors and stay away from "those people" out there who only want to hurt us, or rob us, or perhaps even kill us if they had the chance.

Dr. Deborah Serani, a psychiatrist writing for *Psychology Today*, noted:

> "In previous decades, the journalistic mission was to report the news as it actually happened, with fairness, balance, and integrity. However, capitalistic motives associated with journalism have forced much of today's television news to look to the spectacular, the stirring, and the controversial as news stories. It's no longer a race to break the story first or get the facts right. Instead, it's to acquire good ratings in order to get advertisers, so that profits soar…"[4]

She goes on to explain:

> "Fear-based news programming has two aims. The first is to grab the viewer's attention…The second aim is to persuade the viewer that the solution for reducing the identified fear will be in the news story…What occurs psychologically for the viewer is a fragmented sense of knowing what's real, which sets off feelings of hopelessness and helplessness—experiences known to worsen depression."[5]

When people are afraid, they are easy to manipulate. They are quick to adopt an "us versus them" posture, and will more readily participate in scapegoating—in which an entire people group, political party, religious group, race, or other faction may be pinned with the blame for whatever threat has been identified, whether real or imagined.

In his book, *In the Name of Identity: Violence and the Need to Belong,* author Amin Maalouf accurately identifies tribalism and fear as catalysts for violence and genocide. Throughout history, we can recognize the way those in power have rallied people together under an identity rooted in nationalism, and leveraged that to incite large-scale acts of violence and war. This happens all in the name of identity: one tribe against the other, one religion against another, one nation against the other.

Barry Glassner, author of *"The Culture of Fear: Why Americans Are Afraid of the Wrong Things,"* says:

> "I think there is a fear industrial complex...[which] is composed of politicians, activist groups and corporations that all sell us on the idea that they can provide safety from the very dangers they are scaring us about."[6]

> "Whenever somebody's trying to scare us, the question to ask is 'Are they benefiting from it, and in what way?'" says Glassner. "If they're selling us a product, if they're selling us their political campaign or their cause or whatever it is, we should ask how big is the danger, really? Is it big, is it small, or is it just that they stand to benefit by making us scared?"

And Dr. Edward Hallowell, author of *"Worry: Hope and Help for a Common Condition"* heartily agrees: "Fear gets your eyeballs," he says.

But, is this what Christians are supposed to be like? Are we meant to be ruled by fear? Hardly. In fact, we are told specifically the opposite: "For God has not given us a spirit of fear, but of power and of love and of a sound mind" (2 Timothy 1:7).

Fear and worry are un-Christian practices. How can I say this? Because Jesus says, "therefore I tell you, do not worry about your life" (Matthew 6:25).

Jesus tells us not to worry. If we ignore his instructions and practice worrying instead, then we are disobedient to Jesus.

When we worry, we are saying that we doubt that God is in control. We give power to our fear, and we act as if God isn't big enough to handle our life.

Christians should be immune to these tactics of fear. We have been re-designed by our Creator into new creatures who are motivated by love, not by tribalism, national identity or fear.

Yet, for many Christians in America today, it seems that fear is the main driving force.

I have hundreds of friends on Facebook and Twitter who claim to follow Jesus, and yet they are constantly posting articles and sharing stories about how we need to fear Obama's impending takeover of our nation by force, or about the Jade Helm conspiracy, the blood moon prophecy, or about secret FEMA camps being built to contain Christians when the antichrist eventually rises up to imprison us all.

ALL OF THESE CONSPIRACIES ARE SIMPLY ABOUT EMPLOYING FEAR TO MOTIVATE PEOPLE TO SUPPORT AN AGENDA, GIVE TO A CAUSE, OR POLARIZE A VOTING BLOCK.

Sometimes it feels like a non-stop barrage of "Lions and tigers and bears! Oh, my!" from people who claim to follow the Prince of Peace.

Truthfully, none of this is really new. I remember hearing some of these exact same claims when I was in my twenties—only then the claims were made about Clinton and the liberal agenda. Now they've just recycled the narrative and dropped in Obama's name, because fear motivates.

All of these conspiracies are simply about employing fear to motivate people to support an agenda, give to a cause, or polarize a voting block.

As the date of each pending disaster comes and goes without any incident, you would think that people would eventually wise up. But, they don't. Instead of learning from all of this, it seems that most people will just jump over to the next big conspiracy and scream that "the sky is falling" all over again.

I have a copy of the book, *88 Reasons Why the Rapture Will Occur In 1988,* in my garage. It's full of very convincing reasons (88 of them) but it's also dead wrong. And we could say the same about other failed end-times "prophets" like Harold Camping, Hal Lindsey, or John Hagee and his "Blood Moon" hype.

What concerns me most of all is that Christians are the ones who wave this flag of fear around—and doing so makes us look stupid. It makes us appear irrational. Most of all, it demonstrates to the world that we are driven and motivated by fear.

Again, Jesus commands us not to fear. The New Testament clarifies that fear should not be what motivates us; our inspiration should stem from love. And it's also very clear that you can't be filled with the love of Christ and be fearful at the same time:

> "There is no fear in love. But perfect love drives out fear, because fear has to do with punishment. The one who fears is not made perfect in love" (1 John 4:18).

Our choice is simple: We either decide to remain in a place of fear—and thus make decisions that flow from that fear—*or* we decide to live in the love of Christ and thus make decisions that flow from Him and His love.

Let's not kid ourselves here. We cannot do both. Either we put our hope in Christ and walk in His love, or we walk in fear and live our lives as people who must manage those fears.

Let's consider this for a moment: Could someone who honestly put their hope in Christ ever live in continual fear? Of course not! Someone who is led by their fears can't—at the same time—be completely trusting the Lord and placing their hope in Him. The two are mutually exclusive.

Jesus tells us not to be afraid. He tells us not to fear men, who can only destroy our body but not our soul. He even tells us not to fear Him, but to trust Him and to follow His commands.

If we were honest, we would have to admit that so much of our politics is driven by fear. We're told to fear the liberals, to oppose the gay agenda, and to stand up against any number of enemies whose only aim is to steal our liberties, take away our guns, or otherwise threaten our way of life.

This fear is simply a tool to manipulate us into voting the way they want us to, to send money, or to add our name to a survey. Fear is a tactic, and it's not one that is used by our Lord. Our Lord commands us to rest in Him and trust that He is in control. What's more, He tells us to "seek first the Kingdom of God" and not to worry about tomorrow.

I love what James Douglass says in his book, *The Non-Violent Coming of God,* about the power of fear:

> "Death and the fear of suffering unto death ... serve as the deterrent system of every empire in history. The law of violence is that death is supreme. But if death so rules the world, what about those whose kingdom is not of this world of death? What about those who through interior struggle have been given the grace to overcome the fear of death? What about those who refuse to submit to the law of violence, who refuse to pledge allegiance to the empire of death? For those liberated from the fear of death, the law of violence is powerless. Nonviolence is the overcoming of death by a fearless love."

One reason Christians in America are especially vulnerable to these tactics is due to the fact that, at heart, we have an identity crisis. We don't really know who we are.

That's what we'll look at in our next chapter.

CHAPTER 11

OUR NATIONAL IDENTITY CRISIS

"There are two opposite spirits that have been operative within American Christianity since the beginning of this nation. One is submission. The other is revolution. The one was learned from Jesus, the other from the Enlightenment. This dual spirit explains how guns, the military, soldiering, and Old Glory are virtual sacraments in the life of the American Church. In fact, the average Christian may be more moved to tears by these symbols than they are by baptism, the broken bread and poured out wine, and the preaching of the cross."

– RANCE DARITY

Often when I write about how Christians should do what Jesus said and love our enemies or turn the other cheek, someone will challenge me and ask, "Then what should we do about ISIS?" or "What should we have done about Hitler?"

The question itself reveals their confusion. See, when I say "we should love our enemies, bless those who curse us, and do good to those who hate us," I am talking about "we," the Church. That's the only "we" I know of.

But when other Christians respond by asking "What do we do about ISIS?" they reveal that, to them, "we" equals the State, not the Church.

So, to them, they can't understand how following the commands of Jesus might work when it comes to addressing national threats.

Jesus never meant for his commands to be obeyed by national governments. He was speaking to His followers—the Church. So, if someone identifies themselves more with the State than with the Church, they have placed themselves in a group that is by definition immune to the teachings of Christ.

This came into clear focus for me recently when I was reading the book, *The Reformers and Their Stepchildren,* by Leonard Verduin. In this book, the author explains how the Anabaptists and the Reformers clashed over exactly the same question: "Who are *'we'?* "

The Reformers said that "we" equaled everyone in a given nation. The Anabaptists—in contrast—believed that "we" only pertained to the Church—the Body of Christ—and that the State's authority ended at the doorstep of the *ekklesia.*

This was exactly the mindset of the early Christians as well. They saw themselves as being totally separate from the State, and here's why: Jesus had introduced a revolutionary idea that completely decimated the idea of sacral society.

To understand why this was so revolutionary you have to first understand what is meant by a "sacral society." Sacral doesn't mean "sacrament." It means "bound together by a common religious loyalty."

When Jesus arrived on the scene, he advocated for a radical ideology whereby men and women who differ—both theologically and politically—can still live together in harmony.

As Verduin notes in his book, "this is one of the New Testament's boldest innovations, the sweep of which will not escape the thoughtful."

He continues:

> "It must not escape the reader that this was a novel insight, so novel as to be revolutionary. The world had never seen the like of it before. For all pre-Christian society is sacral."

He goes on to point out that all other ancient societies were pre-Christian, and therefore "sacral." As he explains:

> "The society of ancient Babylon...was a sacral society; all Babylonians were expected to bow to the one and the same "Object" (See Daniel 3); their society was pre-Christian."
> "The society of Ephesus was sacral; all Ephesians were expected to join in the chant: "Great is Diana of the Ephesians!"; (See Acts 19:28) Ephesian society was pre-Christian."
> "In our own day, the society of the Navajo...is sacral; all members of that society are expected to take part in the ritual; theirs, too, is a pre-Christian society."

And then, he drops the proverbial bomb:

> "According to the construction of things, the Old Testament too was pre-Christian—as indeed it was in the chronological sense. Every member of the OT society was considered to be in the same religious category as was every other member of it. *This makes the Old Testament society sacral and pre-Christian.*"

Why is this insight so powerful? Because if those Reformed Christians had understood this simple truth, then the murder of the Anabaptists by their Christian brothers would never have taken place.

> "...there would in all probability never have been a [persecution of Anabaptists] if the Reformers had been aware of the pre-Christian quality of the Old Testament in this matter. It was the Reformer's refusal to admit that there is this perspective in the relationship that obtains between the two Testaments, it was their refusal to grant that the one had outmoded the

other at this point, that caused the exodus of the Stepchildren (Anabaptists)."

So, the Reformers were sacral and therefore they saw themselves as being both Christians and Nationalists. The Anabaptists were non-sacral, having embraced the revolutionary teachings of Jesus that allowed them to identify themselves as followers of Christ alone.

Today's Christians are still very much in the Reformed mindset. Especially those who appear to be pushing—and pushing hard—for a theocratic form of government, where the laws of our land are crafted to coerce everyone (Christian or otherwise) to act like a Christian.

They also tend to see America as a Christian nation and attempt to "bring America back to God"—as if it were ever a nation that was founded on the specific teachings of Jesus.

BECAUSE CHRISTIANS WHO ALIGN THEMSELVES WITH THE STATE HAVE THE POWER OF THE SWORD, HISTORICALLY THEY HAVE USED THAT POWER TO IMPRISON, TORTURE, AND EVEN PUT TO DEATH ANY WHO DISAGREE WITH THEM—EVEN THEIR OWN BROTHERS AND SISTERS IN CHRIST.

This difference in perspective is significant. It's ancient.

It's also deadly.

Because Christians who align themselves with the State have the power of the sword, historically they have used that power to imprison, torture, and even put to death any who disagree with them—even their own brothers and sisters in Christ.

This is also why it is so tragic that Constantine was allowed to undo the revolutionary teaching of Jesus when he entangled the Church and the State and reformed a sacral society of Christians in Rome.

Verduin illustrates beautifully the differences between the sacral perspective of the first century Jews and the radical teaching of Jesus in the Gospel of the Kingdom:

> "It was because the Jews of Jesus' day were pre-Christian, and therefore sacralists in their conception of things, that the problem "whether it is lawful to pay tribute to Caesar" seemed to them an insoluble problem. How could a man, they asked, be loyal to the political community by paying his taxes, without thereby being disloyal to the religious community, the Church? *They, sacralists that they were, knew no answer to this question. It vexed them every time they tangled with it.* And for that reason they confronted the Master with it, so that He too might be embarrassed by it and be hopelessly pinned in a corner. How great must have been their surprise at the ease with which Jesus, acting on the new insight He had come to convey, sailed through the dilemma with "Render unto Caesar what is Caesar's and to God what is God's". *In His way of thinking there wasn't even any problem.*
>
> As the thoughtful reader will have perceived, much is implied in this New Testament innovation. In it is implied that the State is a secular institution… *It is implied in the NT vision that Christianity is not a culture-creating thing, but rather a culture-influencing one.*"

The Church was never meant to be yoked to the State. We are not compelled to legislate culture through the courts or the law. Instead, we are commanded to communicate the radical Gospel of Jesus to everyone around us, and to influence the human heart to submit to the rule and reign of Christ—regardless of what the laws of the land may be.

In that way, Christianity seeks to transform the culture from within rather than to legislate culture from above. As Verduin notes:

> "…there can never be such a thing as a Christian culture; there can only be cultures in which the influence of Christianity is

> more or less apparent. The New Testament vision does not pit a "Christian culture" against a non-Christian culture; rather does it introduce a leaven into any existing culture into which it insinuates itself, a leaven whereby that already existing culture is then affected."

The early church also stood firm against the idea that one could be a Christian and participate in the affairs of the empire or of politics. As Tatian, an early church leader, wrote:

> "I do not wish to be a king; I am not anxious to be rich; I decline military command [and] die to the world, repudiating the madness that is in it."[1]

And as another early Christian writer, Hippolytus of Rome said:

> "A military commander or civic magistrate must resign or be rejected. If a believer seeks to become a soldier, he must be rejected, for he has despised God."

Who are "*we*," then? This question of identity is an important distinction. Do we primarily think of ourselves as patriots and citizens of the nation in which we were born? Or, do we see ourselves as strangers and aliens in this place and citizens of a Kingdom that is above?

If we see ourselves mainly as nationalistic people, then we will act accordingly. Politics will sway us. Wars will inspire us. Economics will influence us.

But if we see ourselves mainly as people of the Kingdom—people who are not of this world—then we will live accordingly. We will be moved by what moves the heart of Jesus. We will be concerned with the things that Jesus was primarily concerned with: love, compassion, service, mercy, justice, and forgiveness. We will be compelled to follow Him and to put His words into practice, no matter what the cost.

This sacral mindset is also the reason why Christians in America often become confused whenever someone says, "Jesus wants us to care for the poor," or "Jesus wants us to love our enemies." To them, these statements have political overtones. They hear the word "us" and assume that this must mean "our nation" rather than "our church," or simply us as individuals.

I have personally been accused of being a liberal for asserting that Christians should care for the poor or refrain from violence. But these are not statements intended to reflect my political opinions. They are the words of Christ!

In short, people who assume that I am being political do so because they are primarily political in their own thinking.

So, again, for the record, I am not a liberal or a Democrat. I am also not a Republican or a Libertarian. I do not even vote. I do not endorse any political party or agenda or candidate for office. I place no faith whatsoever in politics or politicians.

My hope is in Christ and in His Gospel alone. The frustrating thing is that, whenever someone advocates for the idea that Christians should listen to the words of Jesus and put them into practice by caring for the poor, loving their enemy, or refraining from violence they risk being labeled as a liberal or accused of being motivated by politics. Even if what they're really doing is following the Lord Jesus Christ.

As long as Christians maintain a sacral perspective of their faith and their society, they are immunizing themselves to the teachings of Jesus. One cannot help but wonder if this mindset exposes the enemy's tactics against the Body of Christ. As long as Christians embrace this sacral ideology, the Gospel remains unpreached and unlived.

The only hope for this nation—for this entire world—is Jesus Christ and His Gospel of the Kingdom. The only hope for us is to live it out in our daily lives and to put His Kingdom on display for everyone to see.

Sadly, I believe that the Church today is more American than Christian. We are largely unable to divorce our faith from our nationalism.

Those who follow Jesus know that the solution to society's problems will never be found in politics. If we hope to change the hearts of men and women by laws and policies, then we are both mistaken and misguided.

IT DISTURBS ME THAT SO MANY CHRISTIANS I KNOW ARE MORE ACQUAINTED WITH POLITICS THAN THEY ARE WITH THE WORD OF GOD OR WITH FOLLOWING JESUS IN THEIR DAILY LIFE.

Jesus commands us to pledge allegiance to the Kingdom of God, not to a flag or a nation. I'm not saying it's a sin to love your country or to vote, but I am saying that once we blur the lines between Jesus and our national pride, we might have a problem. A big problem.

We are commanded by our Lord to seek first the Kingdom of God and to trust in Him alone—not in the laws of our land or in our political parties.

It disturbs me that so many Christians I know are more acquainted with politics than they are with the Word of God or with following Jesus in their daily life. The decision to surrender your life to Jesus and follow His teachings and example does not make you an American. We have to try to conceptualize—and practice—our faith apart from our patriotism.

So, we must realize that someone can be a Christian without pledging allegiance to the flag or to that nation for which it stands.

Even more importantly, we must strive to see Jesus apart from our cultural, political, and nationalistic filters. This means that our posture towards the poor and the outcast should be inspired by our Lord Jesus, not by our political worldview.

Our hope is in the power of the Gospel to change hearts. It is not in the power of politics to legislate morality. If we're not careful, we will end up succeeding in our quest for power and we will have only created another oppressive theocracy like the one our founding fathers came here to avoid.

At best, even if we were to succeed at creating the perfect government, we will still have failed to obey Jesus and make disciples of all nations.

The governments of this planet are of this world, not of God. Our allegiance is to Jesus alone. His Kingdom is our only true homeland.

So I ask you: Are you an American, or are you a Christian? If you think you can be both, I urge you to carefully reconcile the widely divergent philosophies of Christ and those found in our Constitution.

Americans have the right to be treated equally and to pursue happiness. Christians have only the right to share in the sufferings of Christ, give up their individual identity, and love and serve others as Jesus did.

Americans have the opportunity to vote and choose their leaders. Christians have only one leader, and owe their allegiance to only one, true holy nation—the Kingdom of God.

Ask yourself: "Which of Jesus' teachings were the basis for the American government?" Was it turning the other cheek? Loving your neighbor? Doing good to those who hate you? Blessing those who curse you? Or, maybe it was the Sermon on the Mount or the Great Commission? No, it was none of those things. Therefore, it is difficult to say that America is a "Christian nation" as it was not founded upon the teachings of Jesus.

There is only one holy nation on this earth, and it is us: "But you are a chosen people, a royal priesthood, a holy nation…" (1 Peter 2:9).

Who is the apostle Peter talking to? To the Church. We are the people who are now called "a royal priesthood" and "a holy nation." (Revelation 5:9-10).

Let me ask you this: Would you give up being an American to follow Jesus?

Jesus said we could not follow two masters. He also told us that we should give to Caesar the things that are Caesar's and to God the things that are God's.

What if you cannot serve both Caesar and Jesus? What if you were actually called to live here as "a stranger and an alien" in this country? What if you were an ambassador here who was forbidden to pledge allegiance to another flag or nation? What if you were told not to become entangled with the affairs of this world but to devote yourself completely to Christ and His Kingdom?

If you could only give yourself—your whole self—to either God or Caesar, which would it be?

Can you give God half of yourself? Is it possible to serve both God and the empire?

God is not looking for half-hearted disciples. He demands—and frankly deserves—all of you. Remember, you and I were bought with a price. That price was the death of Christ upon a Roman cross. Your life—all of it—has been bought and paid for long ago.

We don't like to admit it, but Jesus does ask us to give up everything: "In the same way, those of you who do not give up everything you have cannot be my disciples" (Luke 14:33).

Are we more American than Christian? Do we identify more as citizens of the United States than as citizens of the Kingdom of God? We must make a choice. Who is our Lord? To whom do we pledge our total and complete allegiance?

If we refuse to abandon our nationalism, then we align ourselves with "the nations" of this world and with the American empire, both of which stand opposed to Christ and His Kingdom.

If we continue to cling to tribalism, which declares that we are separate from everyone else in the family of God around the globe who is not also in our tribe, then we divide the Body of Christ.

If we love one another as Jesus loved us, we will not treat other Christians with contempt for having different political ideas than we do; we will not look down on other Christians who are of a different race, or who hold to a different theology than we do.

In fact, all of these divisions are evil and are tactics of the enemy to drive the Body of Christ apart. Jesus said that our unity in love would be a sign to the world that we were His disciples. This is why the enemy has worked so hard—and so successfully—to divide Christians over things like doctrine, denominations, nationalism, racism, etc.

What are the greater implications of being a nationalist? Does the scripture have anything to say about it?

You might be surprised.

CHAPTER 12

ONE HOLY NATION

"Patriotism is for the ruled a renunciation of human dignity, reason, conscience, and a slavish submission to those who are in power. Patriotism in its simplest significance is for the rulers nothing but a tool for attaining their ambitious and selfish ends. Patriotism is slavery."

– LEO TOLSTOY[1]

When we examine the New Testament writings, we see that the nations and kings of the earth are at odds with Christ and His Kingdom. The book of Revelation is especially adept at expressing this to us. What we see there is that Jesus is at odds with the kings of the earth, and that the nations come together to make war with Him. We witness the great multitudes being called out "from every nation, tribe, people and language, standing before the throne, in front of the Lamb" (Revelation 7:9).

We also see in John's apocalyptic epistle that everything comes to a close where Jesus is enthroned in the New Jerusalem. We see that, outside the walls of the city, are the nations who opposed Him and attempted to resist His rule over the earth (Revelation chapter 22).

This alone should give us pause. Do we want to stand with Jesus, or with our nation? If we insist on standing with our nation and refuse to abandon our national pride, where does that leave us? Apparently, it leaves us on the outside of the city and separated from Jesus—something that should certainly cause us to question the sanity of nationalism.

JESUS, IN REVELATION, IS SEEN AS A KING WHO IS WAGING WAR WITH THE NATIONS OF THE EARTH. NOT JUST THE "BAD" NATIONS—EVERY NATION. HIS KINGDOM INTENDS TO SUPPLANT AND REPLACE EVERY EARTHLY KINGDOM THAT HAS EVER REIGNED OR WILL EVER REIGN.

Jesus, in Revelation, is seen as a King who is waging war with the nations of the earth. Not just the "bad" nations—every nation. His Kingdom intends to supplant and replace every earthly kingdom that has ever reigned or will ever reign.

In fact, the worthiness of Jesus is directly tied to this reality when the twenty-four elders sing a new song which proclaims of Him:

> "You are worthy to take the scroll and to open its seals, because you were slain, and with your blood you purchased men for God from every tribe, and language and people and nation. You have made them to be a kingdom and priests to serve our God, and they will reign on the earth." (Revelation 5:9-10).

Is Jesus worthy? Yes, He most certainly is. Why? Because Jesus has not only offered Himself on the cross, He has "purchased men for God from every tribe, and language and people and nation."

This means that Jesus has called us out of the nations and He has done so in order to make us "a kingdom of priests to serve our God."

If we refuse to be called out of the nations—if we stand fast, wrapped in the colors and flags of our country, pledging allegiance to it, and sending our sons and daughters to fight for it—then we risk being left outside the city gates when Jesus overcomes the nations of this earth and establishes His eternal Kingdom.

What does our refusal to abandon our nationalism say to Jesus who has suffered and died to rescue us from out of the nations? What does our allegiance to the empires of this world say to the One who died to purchase us as His own? Are we not forsaking our new identity as citizens of a holy nation by maintaining our solidarity with an earthly government ruled by men?

Jesus was very clear:

> "No one can serve two masters. Either he will hate the one and love the other, or he will be devoted to the one and despise the other" (Matthew 6:24).

And the apostles concur:

> "Adulterers and adulteresses! Do you not know that friendship with the world is enmity with God? Whoever therefore wants to be a friend of the world makes himself an enemy of God" (James 4:4).

> "Do not love the world, or anything in the world. If anyone loves the world, the love of the Father is not in him. For everything in the world—the craving of sinful man, the lust of his eyes, and the boasting of what he has and does—comes not from the Father but from the world. The world and its desires will pass away, but the man who does the will of God will live forever" (1 John 2:15-17).

> "Come out of her, my people, so that you will not share in her sins, so that you will not receive any of her plagues; for her sins are piled up to heaven, and God has remembered her crimes" (Revelation 18:4-5).

Let us not forget that Jesus is a King. As the Messiah, He came to announce the coming of His Kingdom upon the earth. The Gospel of the Kingdom that Jesus preached was about the breaking in of His Kingdom upon our planet. The process has already begun, and for the last two thousand years it has continually progressed to fill the earth. His plan is that it will relentlessly advance until it eventually overtakes every person's heart and mind and soul. In this way, Jesus intends to remake the world from within and to subversively transform the world until "the kingdom of the world has become the Kingdom of our Lord and of His Christ, and He will reign forever and ever" (Revelation 11:15).

The Messianic purpose of Jesus is to establish His Kingdom here. We dare not oppose this process or stand in His way. As the prophet Isaiah reminds us, "before Him all the nations are as nothing; they are regarded by Him as worthless and less than nothing" (Isaiah 40:17).

Jesus is fully intent upon making us into a new people, a holy nation that is fully surrendered to His authority and reign in the here and now. Part of our submission to Christ as King is to renounce our identity as citizens of this world, and to embrace our new identity as subjects of God's Kingdom—which is soon to overtake all other kingdoms.

If we insist upon identifying ourselves as Americans, or as members of any group other than those who are fully submitted to Christ, then we place ourselves at odds with Jesus and His Kingdom.

We, like Paul, should resolve to know nothing except Jesus Christ, and Him crucified; and to count all former identities as dung and rubbish, as Paul did when he renounced his Jewish nationalism, his title as a Pharisee, and his tribal heritage saying:

> "Indeed, I count everything as loss because of the surpassing worth of knowing Christ Jesus my Lord. For his sake I have suffered the loss of all things and count them as rubbish, in order that I may gain Christ and be found in him" (Philippians 3:8-9).

Why is it so important to abandon our nationalism? Because once we identify ourselves as an "us," we automatically set ourselves apart from "them," and what follows is an age-old pattern whereby "we" need to gain an advantage over "them", which leads to strife, struggle, violence, and war.

Jesus calls us out of that paradigm. He has come to make all things new—not only to re-make us into new creatures, with new natures, a new heart, and the mind of Christ—but also to form us into a new people with a new citizenship in a new Kingdom with a new King.

This is why Paul, immediately after announcing that he had crucified his connections with the entanglements of nationalism, racism, and religion, said:

> "But our citizenship is in heaven, and from it we await a Savior, the Lord Jesus Christ, who will transform our lowly body to be like his glorious body, by the power that enables him even to subject all things to himself" (Philippians 3:20-21).

Nowhere in the New Testament do we see any hint or suggestion that followers of Jesus are allowed the status of dual citizenship in both His Kingdom and the nation into which we were born. Quite the contrary. Over and over again, the Scriptures proclaim that those who follow Jesus are called out of the nations and into a brand new nation that is from above.

> "So in Christ Jesus you are all children of God through faith, for all of you who were baptized into Christ have clothed yourselves with Christ. There is neither Jew nor Gentile, neither slave nor free, nor is there male and female, for you are all one in Christ Jesus" (Galatians 3:26-28).

> "People who say such things show that they are looking for a country of their own. If they had been thinking of the country they had left, they would have had opportunity to return. Instead, they were longing for a better country—a heavenly

one. Therefore, God is not ashamed to be called their God, for he has prepared a city for them" (Hebrews 11:14-16).

What confuses some Christians—especially those who take a "Flat Bible" approach—is that the Old Testament scriptures appear to speak favorably about Kings like David and Josiah. David is even called "a man after God's own heart" so how can God possibly be against the idea of sanctified earthly leaders or government?

Such questions ignore a very important detail: Kingship was never God's plan. It was the demands of the Israelite people for "a king like all the other nations have" that led to the appointment of kings like Saul, and David and Solomon. In truth, this decision broke God's heart. He saw it as a rejection of Himself as ruler over His people. As God said to the prophet Samuel concerning this, "It is not you they have rejected, but they have rejected me as their king" (1 Samuel 8:7).

So today, when God's people—the Church—place their hopes in political leaders and focus so much energy on elections and legislation, they are doing exactly the same thing; they are forgetting that God is their King and that they do not need to rely on earthly political powers.

Let's not forget that the Messiah is a King. He has come to establish a Kingdom here on this earth. God is asking us to crown Him as our Lord, and that entails shifting our citizenship from the nation where we were born into His Kingdom. He wants to rule and reign—right now—in our actual daily lives. He wants to be our King. He wants us to be His people. It was an awareness of this fact that inspired the early Christians to proclaim "Jesus is Lord!" and to even go to their deaths saying, "We have no King but Jesus."

CHAPTER 13

TRIBALISM AND VIOLENCE

"When Jesus tells us to love our enemies, He probably means that we shouldn't kill them."

– DR. THOMAS CRISP

Our world is filled with violence. It's all over the news. It's in our cities and sometimes even in our own neighborhood and family.

One of the root causes of violence in our world at large, however, stems from tribalism. Throughout human history, acts of violence—war, genocide, terrorism, etc.—have all been done in the name of tribalism. It has been one tribe versus the other tribe; one religion against another religion; one nation against another nation.

Tribalism leads to violence and conflict. The process is simple: I identify myself as being a member of a particular group. Because I am in this group, I see the need to protect others in my group, and I have a strong desire to help my group advance in power, popularity and influence.

This, at the most basic level, creates the "us versus them" mentality. From there, it is a short walk to violence and conflict against "those other people" who are not part of my tribe.[1]

If my identity comes from being part of a certain tribe, then I rejoice when other tribes fail. I laugh when those other tribes lose. I cheer when our tribe wins. I demonize people from that other tribe as being stupid, hateful, or evil. That makes my tribe seem better and their tribe seem worse.

Isn't this exactly what we see and hear on talk radio or political talk shows on TV? Republicans demonize Democrats. Liberals mock Republicans. Every opportunity to belittle the other side is seen as a way to prove that they are right and the others are wrong, and the pattern not only continues—it escalates.

Very soon, I am joining in with others in my group who are working to stop that other tribe from doing something we don't like. Then we get aggressive in our tactics; and before you know it, someone is smearing another person's name or humiliating someone for a mistake they made. As tribalism progresses, it's not difficult to justify throwing a rock or firing a weapon to give our tribe the advantage it deserves.

Jesus understood this. It's why He told the parable of the good Samaritan to Jews—the same Jews who hated Samaritans—when they asked Him to clarify who was the "neighbor" they were commanded to love. In our culture today it could very well be re-told as "The parable of the good homosexual," the "good Muslim," the "good liberal Democrat," etc.

Until we abandon our tribalism, we will never fully understand what Jesus was trying to tell us about what it means to live in His Kingdom.

Simply put, if we ever hope to love our neighbors, we have to be able to step outside of our tribe and see beyond our traditional group identity. In the Body of Christ, there shouldn't be any tribes at all.

This is why Paul did not allow the believers in Corinth to line up behind Peter, behind Apollos, or even behind himself.

Their misguided advocacy for human leaders was creating little factions and tribes within their church.

> "My brothers and sisters, some from Chloe's household have informed me that there are quarrels among you. What I mean is this: One of you says, "I follow Paul"; another, "I follow Apollos"; another, "I follow Peter"; still another, "I follow Christ." Is Christ divided? Was Paul crucified for you? Were you baptized in the name of Paul?" (1 Corinthians 1:11-13).

The point Paul wanted them to understand is quite simple: *Don't align yourself with anyone but Christ.*

If it was wrong for those Corinthian Christians to divide against one another over a preference for an apostle, how in the world would it be acceptable for Christians today to divide against one another over allegiances to this political party or the other? How is it acceptable to divide over this political candidate or that one?

Answer: It's not. *"Is Christ divided?"* No, He is not.

Yet, today, Christians in America are especially divided over politics; and, yes, over this Christian leader or that one. We divide over this doctrine or that denomination. It ought not to be so.

Imagine what might happen if you could honestly strip away every label and scrap of tribal identity? What if you were not a Baptist, but simply someone who loved Jesus?

What if you weren't a Republican or a Democrat anymore, but simply a follower of Christ? What if you abandoned your identity as an American and saw yourself simply as a citizen in the Kingdom of God?

That is exactly what Paul wants us to grasp when he says:

> "For all of you who were baptized into Christ have clothed yourselves with Christ. There is neither Jew nor Gentile, neither slave nor free, nor is there male and female, for you are all one in Christ Jesus" (Galatians 3:27-28).

Casting off our former identities is essential to unity. It's also essential to our mission, which is to love everyone—regardless of nationality, race, religion, sexual orientation, gender, or otherwise.

CASTING OFF OUR FORMER IDENTITIES IS ESSENTIAL TO UNITY. IT'S ALSO ESSENTIAL TO OUR MISSION, WHICH IS TO LOVE EVERYONE—REGARDLESS OF NATIONALITY, RACE, RELIGION, SEXUAL ORIENTATION, GENDER, OR OTHERWISE.

"But," you might say, "isn't being a Christian just another tribe to join?" Maybe, but I am not convinced it has to be.

For example, you can find your identity in Christ without resorting to tribalism. You can see yourself as a citizen of Christ's Kingdom without standing against another nation or kingdom, or religion.

Here's why: Being a member of the Body of Christ, by definition, is to be someone who does not use violence, or dominate others, or seek to put down other people, or take joy when others fail.

Remember, Jesus told us to love our enemies. That means we don't hate them, we don't seek to dominate them, and we certainly don't kill them.[2]

Would you kill someone you loved? Of course not.

We must also remember that Jesus' greatest command was that we should love one another as He has loved us. Because love is our highest command, we hold tight to these facts about love:

> "Love is patient, love is kind. It does not envy, it does not boast, it is not proud. It does not dishonor others, it is not self-seeking, it is not easily angered, it keeps no record of wrongs. Love does not delight in evil but rejoices with the truth. It always protects, always trusts, always hopes, always perseveres" (1 Corinthians 13:4-7).

So, whenever you see people who claim to follow Christ standing up to boast, to be unkind, to dishonor someone from another tribe, or to read aloud a list of their sins and failures, then you're seeing someone who is still entangled in tribalism and still very, very far away from what it means to be "in Christ" and full of love for everyone.

Only a die-hard Republican can mock a Democrat. Only a true liberal can dishonor a conservative. Only a passionate Lutheran can turn a Methodist into his scapegoat. Only a patriotic American can insult a Mexican.

But a Christian—a person who is filled with the agape love of Jesus and transformed by His indwelling presence—cannot do any of those things. Not if he or she is truly "in Christ" and being led by the Holy Spirit.

Tribalism separates us. Denominationalism divides us. Politics split us into opposing factions. But Christ came to bring us together. He has given to us the ministry of reconciliation.

It's time to renounce our Tribalism. My only identity is in Christ. The rest of me died when I took up my cross to follow Him.

> "I have been crucified with Christ and I no longer live, but Christ lives in me. The life I now live in the body, I live by faith in the Son of God, who loved me and gave himself for me" (Galatians 2:20).

Simply put, nationalism is idolatry. It is a denial of Christ and His Kingdom which has come, is now advancing, and will one day overtake the kingdoms of this earth—including the nation into which we were born, and to which we were taught to pledge allegiance.

Now, however, we have a new King and a better country which is from above. Our allegiance is to Christ and His Kingdom which is here and now. As ambassadors of this holy nation, we have been called to bear witness to His righteous government. We are here to proclaim "peace" to the nations and to show them a better way.

Nationalism is based on that primitive tribalism that divides us. It is based on fear, enmity, rivalry, and pride. This is what our enemy thrives on. His plan is to stir up division and to inflame our hearts towards violence, war and bloodshed. This is not who we are now. We are members of a Kingdom not made with human hands—a Kingdom founded on the sacrificial love of the Lamb of God, who died to remove these things from our hearts forever. Jesus died to remake us into people who are no longer swayed by fear, violence, pride, anger, jealousy, or war.

When we say "Jesus Is Lord," we mean that He is King over our life. He is King over this earth. He is the One who can save us—not just spiritually, but practically as a people who are all made in His image.

I love how Benjamin L. Corey says it:

> "Remember: The Kingdom of God is made up of people from every nation, every race, and every language. It's hard to have unity in his Kingdom when a handful of his followers are standing in the corner, waving a flag foreign to the Kingdom and shouting, 'we're number one!'"[3]

The truth is that we are not number one. No nation on earth is number one. No leader or king or politician or political ideology is number one.

Those who pledge their allegiance to Christ and His Kingdom cannot serve two masters. This is especially true since Christ calls us to put our hands and hearts into a work designed to dismantle and tear down everything the nations of this earth are founded on and are working so hard to promote, including individualism, wealth, pride, greed, and consumerism.

Jesus came to remove those earthly divisions and to erase those tribal identities. He calls us to see everyone as our neighbor. He commands us to love beyond labels and borders; beyond race and gender; and beyond doctrine and ideology.

If we are truly "not of this world," then we must do more than wear a t-shirt or buy a bumper sticker. We are called to embody our "other-worldliness" as our daily manifesto of life. Being "in Christ" means we are not of this world, even as He is not of it.

This was our Lord's prayer for us before He went to the cross, as recorded in the Gospel of John:

> "They are not of the world, even as I am not of it. Sanctify them by the truth; your word is truth. As you sent me into the world, I have sent them into the world. For them I sanctify myself, that they too may be truly sanctified. My prayer is not for them alone. I pray also for those who will believe in me through their message, that all of them may be one, Father, just as you are in me and I am in you. May they also be in us so that the world may believe that you have sent me. I have given them the glory that you gave me, that they may be one as we are one— I in them and you in me—so that they may be brought to complete unity. Then the world will know that you sent me and have loved them even as you have loved me" (John 17:16-23).

Being one in Christ is essential to fulfilling our Lord's desire for us as His people. In fact, it is one of the only ways "that the world may believe" that Jesus has come from the Father, and that His love for us is powerful enough to transform us into people who are just like Him in this world.

We must crucify our politics. We must put our hands to the plow and not turn back. Our King commands us. We must obey.

©nakedpastor
Hayward

CHAPTER 14

AMERICA: AN UN-CHRISTIAN EMPIRE

"Don't let anybody make you think God chose America as his divine messianic force to be a sort of policeman of the whole world. God has a way of standing before the nations with justice and it seems I can hear God saying to America 'you are too arrogant, and if you don't change your ways, I will rise up and break the backbone of your power, and I will place it in the hands of a nation that doesn't even know my name. Be still and know that I'm God. Men will beat their swords into plow shafts and their spears into pruning hooks, and nations shall not rise up against nations, neither shall they study war anymore.' I don't know about you, I ain't going to study war anymore."

– DR. MARTIN LUTHER KING, JR.[1]

Every American knows the story. Puritans, Quakers, and other religious refugees made their way to the New World in search of religious liberty and the opportunity to escape the tyranny of the King in their homeland.

They braved starvation, sickness, and brutal hardships to settle in America, where they worked together with their countrymen to establish a settlement. Eventually, they established a thriving community in this harsh new land of opportunity.

But slowly, England tightened its grip on these colonists by levying increasingly unjust and higher taxes—without offering them the appropriate level of governmental representation such taxes should guarantee. Eventually, the colonists could bear the burden no longer.

The American Revolution, led by men who would later become known as the Founding Fathers, was largely fought by Christian men who believed that God was on their side, and that shedding the blood of their former countrymen—in the name of freedom and liberty—was their only option.

But was it? Were there no other options available to them? More to the point, was this revolution something that their Lord and Savior ordained?

Most of them certainly believed so, and most American Christians today assume so as well.

Our national hymns and history books are brimming with glorious allusions to God's great favor on the patriots and minutemen who valiantly fought, killed, and died so that our nation could win freedom from the overbearing British Empire.

Our national monuments praise the sacrifices made by these revolutionaries so that God could establish so great a nation as ours in this world.

Such is the myth of nationalism.

But a very similar situation occurred about two thousand years ago in Palestine. When Jesus arrived on the scene, the Jewish people were suffering under the heavy yoke of Roman taxation and oppression. They also yearned for freedom, and they actively sought their promised Messiah—the Leader who (they thought) would appear by God's providence to rally them together, lead a revolt, and help them overthrow their oppressors, establishing them as "one nation under God."

Yet, when their Messiah arrived, he responded quite differently than they expected:

- He withdrew from the Jews when they tried to make him their king (John 6:15).
- He told them to pay their taxes (Matthew 22:17–21).
- He told them not to resist their oppressors (Matthew 5:39).
- He told them to deliberately go out of their way to help Roman soldiers (Matthew 5:41).
- He told them to love their oppressors and warned that if they refused they could not be called the sons of God (Matthew 5:44–45).[2]

Shockingly, the Jews' promised Messiah was not interested in political freedom. He had not come to bring a regime change in their government, but instead looked to usher in a regime change within their hearts.

SHOCKINGLY, THE JEWS' PROMISED MESSIAH WAS NOT INTERESTED IN POLITICAL FREEDOM. HE HAD NOT COME TO BRING A REGIME CHANGE IN THEIR GOVERNMENT, BUT INSTEAD LOOKED TO USHER IN A REGIME CHANGE WITHIN THEIR HEARTS.

His Kingdom was within them. His Lordship was over their heart, not over their national interests. He came to establish his throne in their daily life, not in the throne room of Caesar.

After Christ's death, even as the early Christians increasingly endured persecution under the pagan Roman Empire, their posture was not violent. They understood that they were ambassadors of another Kingdom that was far more powerful and vast.

Yet, they did not seek to promote that Kingdom through force or by political influence. Instead, the apostle Paul encouraged them by saying:

> "Let every person be subject to the governing authorities, for there is no authority except by God, and those that exist are put in place by God. So then, the one who resists authority resists the ordinance which is from God, and those who resist will receive condemnation on themselves" (Romans 13:1–2).

As my friend Chuck McKnight so eloquently noted:

> "Don't forget, when Paul wrote this, he specifically had in mind the corrupt and unjust authority of Rome. If Paul instructed followers of Christ to willingly remain under Roman oppression, it's obvious how he would have reacted to the colonists' break from Great Britain. Let there be no doubt, the American Revolution was first and foremost an act of rebellion against God."[3]

If Jesus warned the Jews not to fight, but to overcome evil with good and to love and serve their oppressors (who were blasphemous, pagan outsiders) how can we possibly justify the violent revolution led by mostly Christian people against their own government?

One reason for our justification is that our revolution was successful, whereas the Jewish revolt ended in the absolute and total devastation of their temple, their priesthood, and their way of life.

If our revolution had ended in similar fashion, no doubt the story would be different. We, as British subjects, would have considered such revolutionaries as traitors. We would no doubt point to those people as examples of what happens to people who dare to defy the sovereignty of our nation or the authority of our leaders.

But, since the American revolution ended with a Colonial victory, we tell the story much differently. We make those revolutionaries our heroes. We praise them for their bravery and foresight. We applaud their dedication to freedom and liberty. We even write songs and sing loudly of our God's great favor and blessing on our nation, as if the bloodshed we were born from was baptized from on high.

But these are merely the echoes of nationalistic pride and patriotic rhetoric designed to obscure the truth, which is that no follower of Jesus has any blessing from God to violently oppose their government in the name of freedom, liberty, or justice.

Unfortunately, many Christians in America today wrongly assume that they live in a Christian nation and that God has blessed America in a way that He has not blessed other nations.

However, no nation on earth is "Christian" because to be a Christian nation is to be "like Christ," and no nation has yet put the teachings of Jesus into practice.

Christian nations do not enslave other races like early American settlers and landowners did. Christian nations do not attempt to systematically exterminate native peoples in order to take over their land and exploit their resources, as the American people did for years. Christian nations do not purposely infect women and children with smallpox by giving them blankets that they know carry the disease, as we did to the Native Americans. Christian nations do not tolerate the abuse, torture, and killing of Christians by other Christians who disagree on their theology, as American Puritans did to American Quakers in the mid 1600s.

And so on, and so on.

Take this analogy, for example: Imagine you live in a huge mansion. One day you discover that there's an entire wing of the building you didn't know was there before. You begin to explore and find a large family that's been living there a long time. They've got nice stuff over there, some of it better than yours.

So, you go over there, kill some people, enslave the survivors, and take their property.

Is that what a Christian would do? No. But that is essentially what the first American settlers did to the Native Americans. That is also what we continue to do in Africa, the Middle East, South America, and other Third World countries today.

America, like every other nation on earth, is man-made and built upon the principles that every nation is built upon.

The goal of this nation is to advance, thrive, and become more powerful. This may only be accomplished if other nations diminish and grow weaker.

While we may say that America has many positive qualities as compared to other nations, we must admit that America is no more like Christ than France, Belgium, and Afghanistan are like Christ. That is to say, America is not at all like Him.

WE DON'T LIKE TO ADMIT IT, BUT AMERICA SPENDS MORE OF ITS MONEY ON CREATING INSTRUMENTS OF DEATH THAN ANY OTHER NATION ON EARTH—MORE THAN THE OTHER SEVEN LARGEST NATIONS COMBINED.

If we are truly honest with ourselves, we can see that the America we want to believe in is not the America that actually exists.

America is not the messenger of Jesus. America, to many of those who live outside our borders, is the messenger of death.

We don't like to admit it, but America spends more of its money on creating instruments of death than any other nation on Earth—more than the other seven largest nations combined.[4] Also, since 1776, America has been waging war somewhere in the world for 214 out of 235 years.[5]

Even worse, America's love for war is so great that often her own children starve[6] so that even more weapons can be built.[7]

This is exactly why Martin Luther King, Jr. said, "America is the greatest purveyor of violence in the world today."[8] Truthfully, without the U.S., the world would be far less violent. Let's face it: America is an empire. Like all empires, America rules by death, fear, and the power of the sword all while pretending she is for freedom and truth and democracy. America maintains more than 800 military bases around the globe at a cost of nearly 100 billion dollars a year.[9] She has more power than Rome ever had. She has the capacity to kill more people around the world than Rome ever dreamed of. She exploits poor nations around the world and rules by intimidation and fear.[10]

America is nothing like Jesus. She is not Christ-like. America will kill women and children for political gain.[11] America will exploit the poor to build greater wealth for herself.[12]

By her actions, America has shown that it believes if it can kill enough people, the world may become a better place. This is not like Christ.

America, then, does not love freedom. America loves money. America's true God is not Jesus. Her only gods are comfort, safety, and luxury. War and death have been in the heart of America since the beginning.

What's worse, our dear sons and daughters are sent by the thousands to die on foreign soil so that our richest corporations[13] may earn billions more in profits.[14] The rich get richer. The poor die or get poorer.

If we dare to look closely, and to be honest, we will see that America is not Christian. If anything, America is closer to what God describes in the book of Ezekiel as being guilty of the sin of Sodom:

> "Behold, this was the sin of your sister Sodom: she and her daughters had arrogance, abundant food and careless ease, but she did not help the poor and needy. Thus they were proud and committed abominations before Me. Therefore, I removed them when I saw it" (Ezekiel 16:49-50).

Should Christians embrace such an American empire? Is there any room for a follower of the Prince of Peace to pledge allegiance to such a violent, greedy and prideful nation as this?

> "Do not be bound together with unbelievers; for what partnership have righteousness and lawlessness, or what fellowship has light with darkness? Or what harmony has Christ with Belial, or what has a believer in common with an unbeliever? Or what agreement has the temple of God with idols? For we are the temple of the living God..." (2 Corinthians 6:14-16).

When we align ourselves with the empire, or any nation, we compromise our identity as the Body of Christ and as citizens of Christ's Kingdom.

Allegiance to our nation means becoming entangled with the politics of that nation, which distracts us from our true mission. Nationalism requires that we take up arms to defend our nation's borders or interests, and this means denying what Jesus commanded us concerning love for our enemies.

I believe we can learn something from the conversion experience of Paul, the apostle, who began as a persecutor of the Church, formerly going by the name "Saul of Tarsus."

Saul thought he was doing God a service by travelling from place to place in order to arrest Christians. Sometimes this "ministry" involved standing by while these Christians were brutally beaten or stoned to death. But for him, these were necessary steps to ensure that those who held differing religious opinions were silenced.

Then, something incredible happened. Jesus appeared to him on the road to Damascus and knocked him to the ground. The words Jesus spoke to him in that moment are especially profound: "Saul, Saul, why are you persecuting Me? It is hard for you to kick against the goads'" (Acts 26:14).

Here, Jesus explains to Paul [Saul] that whenever he does harm to someone who is in Christ, he is actually causing harm to Jesus, too. Keep this in mind: If anyone does harm to another Christian, then they are doing harm to Jesus.

It doesn't matter if we try to justify our violence by saying, "But Jesus, those Christians were disagreeing with my theology," or "those Christians were soldiers fighting for the other side."

Paul was involved in violent persecution against his own Jewish people in the name of his religion. If this isn't acceptable behavior—for a non-believer to violently oppose a Christian—then how could we possibly justify violence against Christians *by other Christians?*

It certainly doesn't matter if we attempt to validate our aggression by claiming that the Christians against whom we fight are citizens of another nation.

THE TRUTH IS, IT DOESN'T MAKE ANY DIFFERENCE TO JESUS IF OUR REASONS FOR HURTING, SHOOTING, BOMBING, OR KILLING OUR BROTHERS AND SISTERS IN CHRIST ARE BASED ON RELIGION, NATIONALISM, OR ANYTHING ELSE.

The truth is, it doesn't make any difference to Jesus if our reasons for hurting, shooting, bombing, or killing our brothers and sisters in Christ are based on religion, nationalism, or anything else. Simply put, we are not allowed to harm a brother or sister in Christ for any reason. There is no excuse for doing so.

According to Jesus, whenever we do harm to another Christian, we are causing Him pain as well.

That means that we, as followers of Christ, are not allowed to justify violence against other Christians by claiming that we're simply following orders, fighting for justice, or standing up for liberty.

When Christians participate in combat, there's no way of knowing if the people we are about to shoot, bomb, or kill are members of our own Christian family.

Remember the story at the beginning of this book, in which one Christian man shot another Christian man after reading Scripture together and praying for one another? Only by embracing nationalism is such an evil ever justified. Without nationalism, violence like this would be unthinkable. Shooting our brothers and sisters in Christ is the same as shooting Jesus. "Whatever you have done to the least of these, my brothers, you have done it unto me" (Matthew 25:40).

But, if we remain neutral in matters of war, then shooting Jesus is never an issue for us. We run no risk of accidentally killing another member of Christ's Body—and thereby hurting Christ in the process—if we refuse to take up arms against another nation.

Unfortunately, as long as we continue to pledge allegiance to our flag, there will be wars. But the followers of Jesus should never kill to protect a symbol or an ideal. Like the early Christians, we should lay down our lives for one another and love our enemies, even if it kills us.

I realize that you might ask, "What about when the war is just? Aren't there certain evils which demand violent intervention? Shouldn't Christians be willing to go to war to stop those evils from being done?"

Some would say yes, but I am not so sure.

CHAPTER 15

JUST WAR?

"I find it interesting that nations fight wars for all the things Jesus said we had to let go of if we wanted to follow Him."

– KENN STILGER

Above all other wars in human history, World War II alone stands as the primary (if only) example of what a just war could look like. Laying aside for a moment whether or not you believe that a just war is even possible, let's look at the fruit of this "just war." What did it produce, other than the eventual end of Nazi Germany?

- The development of nuclear weapons
- The death of 80,000 people in Hiroshima
- Another 60,000 dead due to radiation poisoning
- 73,000 killed in Nagasaki
- Another 70,000 after that due to radiation
- 50 plus years of Cold War escalation as nuclear weapons proliferated between the US and Soviet Russia
- A total of over 70 million fatalities

Let's remember that America did not enter the war in order to stop Hitler. This nation knew all about what Hitler was doing to his people and did nothing. In fact, if it were not for the fact that Japan dared to bomb Pearl Harbor, it is doubtful that the United States would ever have considered entering the war at all.

So, if we are honest, we will admit that America only entered the war when it was about defending national pride, not because the lives of innocents were at stake.

Even more alarming is the fact that America could have ended the Holocaust, and the War, without firing a single shot.

Allow me to explain.

At the start of World War II, the largest oil company in the world was Standard Oil of New Jersey. When I say "they were the largest," I mean that they controlled almost 85 percent of the U.S. petroleum market.

The owners of Standard Oil were the Rockefellers, and the next largest stockholder was a large German chemical company known as I.G. Farben. During the rise of Naziism, there were several reciprocal investments between German and American companies. I.G. Farben was a lucrative financial partner to have.

Through their ingenuity, I.G. Farben enabled Germany to thrive. They had dozens of laboratories and factories which churned out raw materials other German companies couldn't provide—like gasoline, oil, rubber, nitrates, and fibers—all extremely necessary for a nation gearing up for war.

Enticed by the free labor afforded to them through prisoners in the concentration camps, I.G. Farben built a huge industrial complex designed to produce synthetic rubber and oil. It was called "Auschwitz," and it consumed as much electricity as the entire city of Berlin.[1]

Not only did Standard Oil embrace I.G. Farben, so did other American corporations like Du Pont and General Motors.

However, Standard Oil's ties to the Nazis went far beyond their ties to I.G. Farben. Many historians have remarked that without the direct assistance of Standard Oil, the Nazi air force would never have flown.[2]

Why is that? Because the German Air Force, or Luftwaffe, required a very specific kind of gasoline—tetraethyl leaded gasoline—to fuel its engines. At that time, only Standard Oil, Du Pont, and General Motors had the wherewithal to produce it, and it was Standard Oil who supplied it directly to the German Air Force.[3]

But that's not all. In 1941, the U.S. State Department produced a detailed report showing that Standard Oil operated refueling stations in Mexico, Central America, and South America which serviced German and Italian vessels. However, no action was taken against Standard Oil.

MANY AMERICAN SOLDIERS WERE SHOCKED TO DISCOVER THAT THE GERMAN TRUCKS DRIVEN BY THE NAZIS WERE MANUFACTURED BY THE FORD MOTOR COMPANY AND BY OPEL—A GENERAL MOTORS COMPANY WHICH ALSO BUILT GERMAN WAR PLANES.

Lest you think Standard Oil was partial to assisting the Nazis, they also had a similar arrangement providing tetraethyl lead gasoline to fuel Japanese war machines.[4]

Many American soldiers were shocked to discover that the German trucks driven by the Nazis were manufactured by the Ford Motor Company and by Opel—a General Motors Company which also built German war planes.

For his "distinguished service to the Reich," Henry Ford accepted the Grand Cross of the German Eagle—the highest medal that Nazi Germany could award to a foreigner—in July of 1938. James Mooney, a senior executive for General Motors, received his medal a month later.[5]

Not only did these American companies grow rich off Germany's war machine, they did so while resisting pleas from the American President Roosevelt to increase military production for the U.S. Army, according to government documents.[6]

As a sad postscript to all of this, I.G. Farben also supplied another essential item to the Nazis. They created a gas known as "Zyklon-B" which was used to gas millions of Jews in the camps. Evidence shows that the executives at I.G. Farben knew full well how and why that gas was being used.[7]

Because of these things, sadly, America had the power to stop Hitler in his tracks without firing a single shot. If the corporate executives at Standard Oil, General Motors, or Du Pont had wanted to, they simply could have stopped selling tetraethyl lead gasoline to the Germans. This would have grounded every German fighter plane, bomber, and transport. The Allies would have won in a landslide, and perhaps millions of Jews would not have been put to death.

However, this "just war" didn't end that way. It went on and on as a few people got rich—but many, many others fought, suffered, and died.

World War II was the deadliest conflict in human history. It brought about millions of deaths. It created the atomic monster that continues to plague our world and threatens still to blow up the planet ten times over.

Is that what a "just war" looks like? Is this, the best of all possible wars, really something we want to emulate?

The enormous costs associated with World War II should compel us to rethink the very idea of war itself, and to become desperate to find peaceful means to resolve future conflicts.

As followers of Jesus, the Prince of Peace, we need to become experts in peace. We must take seriously the promise of Jesus when he said, "Blessed are the peacemakers for they shall be called the sons of God." (Matthew 5:9)

Are we peacemakers? And if not, are we really followers of Jesus?

Our Lord Jesus equated love with obedience:

> "If you keep my commands, you will remain in my love, just as I have kept my Father's commands and remain in his love. I have told you this so that my joy may be in you and that your joy may be complete. My command is this: Love each other as I have loved you" (John 15:10-12).

The idea of loving others can be challenging, especially when it comes to loving our enemies.

Many Christians want to wiggle out of Jesus' command to love our enemies. We want to redefine love, look for different meanings of the word "kill," or make amendments for self-defense and for defending the innocent.

Then, quite often, Christians will bring up the Holocaust or the Nazis in World War II and ask, "Why didn't non-violence stop Hitler?"

Here's something almost no one realizes: The Nazis had no way of dealing with those who responded with non-violent resistance.

> "B.H. Liddell-Hart, widely acknowledged as the foremost military writer of our times, discovered in his interrogation of Nazi generals after World War II that they had little trouble dealing with violent resistance except in mountainous areas of Russia and the Balkans, or where advancing armies were close. But they expressed complete inability to cope with nonviolence as practiced in Denmark, Holland, Norway, and, to a lesser extent, in France and Belgium.
>
> They were experts in violence, and had been trained to cope with opponents who used that method. But other forms of resistance baffled them. They were relieved when nonviolence was mixed

> with guerilla operations, which made it easier to combine suppressive action against both at the same time.'
>
> The generals found friendly noncompliance more frustrating than any other form of resistance, and had no effective means to counter it. 'If practiced with a cheerful smile and an air of well-meaning mistake, due to incomprehension or clumsiness, it becomes even more baffling... *This subtle kind of resistance cannot really be dealt with in terms of force: indeed, nothing can deal with it. There is really no answer to such go-slow tactics.*'"[8]

IF JESUS SAYS WE SHOULD LOVE OUR ENEMY, THE ANTICHRIST SAYS WE SHOULD TORTURE THEM. IF JESUS COMMANDS US TO BLESS THOSE WHO CURSE US, THE ANTICHRIST URGES US TO MAKE WAR AGAINST THEM.

So, is it really reasonable to say that non-violence couldn't have stopped Hitler's army, especially if his generals had no answer for it?

At best, we might say that we don't know if non-violence could have stopped the Nazis because so few ever attempted it.

In the New Testament, we are told that there is already an antichrist in the world, and that the antichrist is about more than the coming of a future, evil dictator. It's about a spirit that denies Christ's teaching:

> "Dear children, this is the last hour; and as you have heard that the antichrist is coming, even now many antichrists have come" (1 John 2:18).

An antichrist is anyone who denies Christ and goes against His teaching. If Jesus is the Prince of Peace, the antichrist is the Prince of War. If Jesus heals, the antichrist sheds blood.

If Jesus says we should love our enemy, the antichrist says we should torture them. If Jesus commands us to bless those who curse us, the antichrist urges us to make war against them. If Jesus says we should pray for those who persecute us, the antichrist says we ought to oppress and imprison them. If Jesus tells us to care for the poor, the antichrist says we should just ignore them. If Jesus says his disciples will not fight, the antichrist encourages us to glorify violence. If Jesus says we should turn the other cheek, the antichrist says we should destroy the aggressor.

Which of these sounds most like the god that America follows? Who does the Church most resemble today? Are we of Christ, or are we of the antichrist?

The idea of a violent, nationalistic Messiah blinded the Jews from seeing "the things that make for peace." The same idea still blinds us today.

Brothers and sisters, let us repent of our violence and forever lay aside all weapons of war.

Remember, it was not the godless citizens of Jerusalem who killed Jesus. It was those who were deeply religious and believed in using violence in the name of God and country.

We can't say we follow the "Prince of Peace" while saluting the flag of a conquering nation, while cheering for war, or by calling for vengeance. We can't follow Jesus while dismissing His words, for He said to Peter, "Put away your sword. Those who live by the sword will die by the sword."[9] This same Jesus said "Love your enemies," and "If my Kingdom were of this world, my disciples would fight."[10] He said, "Blessed are the peacemakers," and He told us that those who seek to call down fire on their enemies "do not know what spirit (they) are of." This is the Jesus who gave us all "the ministry of reconciliation."

Either Jesus was a fool who taught nonsensical ideals that cannot work in this world, or he was the Son of God who came to teach us another way to think and live; gave us a new blueprint to follow; and ended his sermon on loving our enemies by asking, "Why do you call me 'Lord, Lord' and don't do what I say?"

Our New Testament was written by a violent man who went from house to house, killing and persecuting Christians on behalf of the religious elite. That man, Saul, lived a violent life with the blessing of the empire until Jesus transformed him into an apostle who taught the Gospel of peace. When Jesus transformed him, Saul became Paul and followed Jesus the rest of his life, until he was eventually put to death by that same empire.

Do you want blood? Do you want vengeance for the evils done to you? Jesus says, "Here, take my blood, shed by that same empire of violence and retribution you salute, and to which you pledge allegiance. Here, drink my blood until it transforms your heart into one like mine, which cries out, "Father, forgive them, for they know not what they do!"

We cannot kill our way to peace. Someone has to welcome the enemy and return love for hate. Someone has to lay down his or her weapon first and be the one who is willing to die—but not kill—in order to make this world a better place.

We have forgotten our heritage. We have ignored three hundred years of Christ-following martyrs who obeyed the teachings of Jesus, valiantly loving, serving, and blessing the very same Romans who put them to death.

In the Church today, we no longer resist the empire. Instead, we now embrace that same spirit of the worldly kingdom which killed the martyrs and even our own Lord Jesus.

The deadly virus of the empire has enslaved and bewitched the world. The Kingdom of God is the only cure.

"Come out of her, my people," Jesus says. Stop fornicating with the empire of violence and retribution. "You know not the Spirit you are of."

We are called to repentance. We are commanded to rethink reality from Christ's perspective. He did not come to give us more of the same, but to make all things new. For too long we have compromised our faith by combining it with politics. In the end, we have ended up with politics and very little of the faith that resembles Christ.

What can we do now?

CHAPTER 16

LIVING UNTANGLED

"One of the biggest freedoms I experienced in my Christian walk was when I walked away from caring about who was president. Try it this election cycle and see what happens. Opt out of the arguing, debating and stress of it all—opt out of participating entirely—and tithe all of that time and emotional energy back into the things that God asked us to be busy doing…loving, serving, and pouring ourselves out for His other-worldly Kingdom. You might be surprised at how life-giving it is to abandon the politics of secular empires."

– BENJAMIN L. COREY[1]

If you've made it this far into the book, I want to thank you for sticking with me all the way to the end.

I can only imagine what you might be thinking. Maybe you're feeling a strange sense of freedom now that the burdens of politics and nationalism have been lifted off of your shoulders. Maybe you feel angry because you feel as if I've attacked your beloved nation. Maybe you feel sick to your stomach because you now realize that the America you once believed in isn't as beautiful or as holy as you once hoped.

Whatever you're feeling or thinking, I want you to know that I've been there myself. This is a path that I have walked down already over the last several years of my life.

I have felt the anger when someone criticized my nation. I have felt the sickness in my stomach when I began to realize that the America I had believed in wasn't all I had hoped it was. I have also felt the sense of freedom and sincere relief upon finally accepting that Jesus always had the best solution to the world's problems all along.

Hopefully, you are convinced of this as well. If I have accomplished what I set out to do, then you've had many of your illusions about politics dispelled. If I was successful in helping you to untangle your faith from your politics and nationalism, you might now be asking yourself a few questions, like "What do I do now?"

PARADIGM SHIFTS LIKE THESE TAKE TIME; AND HONESTLY, ONLY THE HOLY SPIRIT CAN TRANSFORM US FROM WITHIN.

Here's what I would suggest: Go back to the Gospels. Open them up and read them again. Listen carefully to the voice of Jesus. Let Him speak to you, and take time to talk with Him about what He is saying—and about how you can put His words into practice.

That's just the beginning.

But there are also a few things I would ask you *not* to do. First, please do not make it your mission to argue with other Christians about how wrong they are to mix their faith and their politics. I know it will be tempting to share your "newfound wisdom" with others, but please remember that your journey hasn't been an easy one. Most likely these convictions have come to you slowly and with much difficulty. Paradigm shifts like these take time; and honestly, only the Holy Spirit can transform us from within.

Even more importantly, please don't look down upon our brothers and sisters in Christ who are still entangled. Don't get angry with those who pledge allegiance to the flag or who confuse their political party with the Kingdom of God. Don't treat Christians in the military as if they are not "true Christians." Don't act as if those who vote are less spiritual than you are.

Why? Because you and I were hopelessly entangled ourselves, not that long ago. Remember that we once pledged allegiance to the flag, and were confused about where our faith ended and our nationalism began.

We are all in process. Some are farther along than others on the curve. We should not assume that we are always perfectly right about anything. Grace is what helps us to love one another in spite of our differences. So, please, extend the same grace to others that you would have wanted them to extend to you.

Now, that doesn't mean that we don't work to untangle our brothers and sisters from their politics and nationalism. It simply means that we work to untangle them by loving them right where they are in their process.

By all means, share this book with your friends and family members who are entangled. I'm happy to play the "bad cop" in this untangling process. But don't become the bulldog yourself.

Instead, look for ways to help our dearly loved brothers and sisters ask themselves questions about their faith and their politics. Try to be as winsome and as gracious as possible every step of the way.

Above all, your own life should reflect the beauty of an untangled reality. Allow them to see you enjoying the freedom of a life untangled from the ways of this world. Show them what an uncompromising faith in Christ looks like, up close and personal. Put the untangled life on display for them every chance you get, but be sure to do so with humility and grace. Love others no matter what, and pray for the Holy Spirit to lead them into total freedom and joyous commitment to our one true King.

Lastly, make sure you focus most of your energy on actually being untangled, rather than trying to untangle others.

In other words, living a life demonstrating your own freedom from nationalism will be more effective at helping others to become untangled themselves than any other tactic you might employ.

Our lives should be so different—so radically like Jesus—that even our brothers and sisters who are entangled might begin to take notice. “Why don’t you vote?” they might ask. “Why don’t you pledge allegiance to the flag?” they will wonder. “Why don’t you believe in violence?”

Hopefully we will not miss the opportunity to give an answer for this hope that lies within us. What else could inspire us to live a life so different from those around us? Only the radiant love of Jesus could permeate our souls so completely and compel us to walk the narrow path of peace with such hopeful abandon.

If our unwavering allegiance to Jesus and His Gospel is capable of transforming our world from within, it is also powerful enough to transform us into His image. As we ourselves change, eventually even our neighbors, family, and friends will want to become people whose hearts are more fully devoted to Christ.

I have dear friends and family members who are still entangled. I’m sure you do, too. Let’s pray together that the Lord Jesus might set them free and open their eyes to the glorious sufficiency of Christ and His glorious Kingdom.

Our hope is not in our nation. We place no faith in politics or policies. Our eyes are set on Jesus. We are looking for a better country. Our goal is to follow our King as obedient ambassadors of Christ.

So, if you want to live an untangled life, here's what I recommend: Don't allow yourself to become deceived again about the need to vote for the right candidate. Remember, Christians have more than enough power at their disposal to change their nation, and it's much more effective than casting a vote once every four years. Or, to put it another way, presidents and politicians have much *less* power than the average Christian when it comes to transformation.

Take that in. We already have *all the power we need* to save our country. The Gospel of Jesus is still the most effective weapon against evil, corruption, violence, hate, fear, and every other sin known to mankind. If you really believe that, don't give in to the fear-based rhetoric that threatens to distract you.

Instead, start sharing the Good News of the Kingdom. Let everyone know that Jesus is the best Leader anyone could ever have. Make sure you remind them that He loves them, and that He would rather die than live without them. Give them an opportunity to become ambassadors for Him.. Teach the people around you to follow Jesus daily, and show them how to put His words into practice.

THE GOSPEL OF JESUS IS STILL THE MOST EFFECTIVE WEAPON AGAINST EVIL, CORRUPTION, VIOLENCE, HATE, FEAR, AND EVERY OTHER SIN KNOWN TO MANKIND. IF YOU REALLY BELIEVE THAT, DON'T GIVE IN TO THE FEAR-BASED RHETORIC THAT THREATENS TO DISTRACT YOU.

If you do this, then you may soon begin noticing that your community, and eventually your nation, are both becoming more Christ-like as the influence of Jesus continues to expand.

This is how we make a nation great: not by casting a vote for a politician that is corrupt, selfish, dishonest, and absolutely incapable of bringing lasting change, but by declaring with our entire life that Jesus is King.

If He is your Lord, cast your vote for Him and begin campaigning for His election.

Remember, the kingdoms of this world are fading away. Our King is coming soon. When He returns, may He find us already living as citizens under His glorious rule.

Amen.

APPENDIX

REVOLVING DOOR POLITICS

The following charts illustrate the revolving door between big business and big government, where those who run the corporations and those who run the government are the same people who rotate in and out of the two seats of power. For more information on Revolving Door Politics and to access up-to-date data, please visit www.opensecrets.org/revolving/

	TRUMP CAMPAIGN	BIG BUSINESS
Paul Manafort	Campaign Chairman	Lobbyist, Ferdinand Marcos
Jim Murphy	National Political Director	Lobbyist, Myanmar Republic
John Mashburn	Policy Director	Lobbyist, Reynolds America Tobacco
Doug Davenport	Delegate Strategist	Lobbyist, Gtech
Mike Mcsherry	Advisor	Lobbyist, Alcoa

	BIG OIL	FEDERAL GOVERNMENT
Andrew Zausner	Dir, Gov't Relations (Pennzoil)	Dept. of Energy (Carter)
Kevin Avery	Dir, Federal Gov't Affairs (Marathon)	Staff: US Rep Landrieu (D)
Jason Schendle	Washington Rep (API)	Staff: US Rep Landrieu (D)
William Ichord	VP, Int'l Gov't Affairs (Conoco Phillips)	Staff: Sen Rockefeller (D) & Biden (D)
James E. Williams	Products Issues Manager (API)	Staff: Sen Durbin (D) & Biden (D)
Matt Gobush	Comm. Manager (ExxonMobil)	Staff: Sen Lieberman (D)
Mark Rubin	Upstream Gen. Manager (API)	Staff: Sen Johnson (D)
Wendy Kirchoff	Dir, Fed Resources (IPAA)	Staff: Rep Kilpatrick (D) & Boren (D)
Rachel Miller	Dir, Fed Affairs (BP America)	Staff: Sen Feinstein (D)
Emily Olson	Lobbyist (BP America)	Staff: Rep D Lipinski and B Lipinksi (D)
Judith Blanchard	Fed Gov't Relations (Chevron)	Dep Staff Director, HGRC (Clinton)
Donna Steele Flynn	Tax Counsel (IPAA)	Dir, House Ways and Means (Clinton)
Lee Fuller	VP, Gov't Relations (IPAA)	Dir, SEPWC (Clinton)
Shirley Neff	Economist (Shell Oil)	Staff Economist SENRC (Clinton)
Theresa Fariello	VP, Gov't Relations (ExxonMobil)	DA Sec, Dept of Energy (Clinton)
Steven Koonin	Chief Scientist (BP)	US: Energy for Science, DOE (Obama)

	PHARMACEUTICALS	FEDERAL GOVERNMENT
Catherine Bennett	VP, Gov't Relations (Pfizer)	National Security Council (Ford)
Michael Pollard	OPA (Pharm Manufacturers Assn)	Fed Trade Commission (Carter)
Dennis DiConcini	Pfizer Legal Counsel (Parry & Romani)	US Senator (D)
Dick Gephardt	Lobbyist (Medicines Co)	US Representative (D)
Kimberly Davis	Corporate Counsel, Lobbyist (Pfizer)	Legislative Asst to Rep Boxer (D)
Desiree Filippone	VP, Int'l Gov Affairs (Eli Lilly)	Sr Policy Advisor to Sen Bayh (D)
Walter Moore	Dir, Congress Relations (Pfizer)	Special Asst to Sen Bentsen (D)
Billy Tauzin	CEO (PhRMA)	US Representative (D)
Geralyn Ritter	VP, Global Public Policy (Merck)	US Trade Representative (Clinton)
Michael Friedman	Sr VP, Public Policy (Pharmacia)	Commissioner, FDA (Clinton)
Raul Perea-Henze	Global Regulatory Policy (Merck)	Asst Sec, Commerce Dept (Clinton)
Caleb DesRosiers	Director, Public Policy (Pfizer)	Medicare Regulatory Affairs (Bush)
Alan Holmer	CEO (PhRMA)	US Treasury Dept (Bush)
Jeffrey Kindler	CEO (Pfizer)	NY Federal Reserve Bank (Obama)
Suresh Kumar	VP, Consumer Products (Pfizer)	USFCS Commerce Dept (Obama)
James Schlicht	Gov't Relations (Bristol-Myers Squibb)	Nat'l Inst of Health (Obama)

	BIG TOBACCO	FEDERAL GOVERNMENT
Andrew Zausner	Lobbyist (Lorillard)	Exec Assistant, DOE (Carter)
Peter Kadzik	Lobbyist (Cigar Assn of America)	Presidential Transition Team (Clinton)
Tanya Lombard	Lobbyist (Philip Morris)	White House Staff (Clinton)
Kirk Blalock	Dir, External Affairs (Philip Morris)	White House Staff (Bush)
Robin Tallon	Lobbyist (Altria Group)	US Rep (D)
Victor Crawford	Lobbyist (Tobacco Institute)	Maryland State Senator (D)
Wendell Ford	Lobbyist (Cigar Assn of America)	US Senator (D)
Robert Mangas	Lobbyist (Cigar Assn of America)	Chief of Staff: Sen Ford (D)
Patrick Raffaniello	Lobbyist (Cigar Assn of America)	Staff: Rep Brewster (D)
Allen Shofe	Dir, Fed Gov't Affairs (Williamson)	Chief of Staff: Rep Gutknecht (R)
John Fish	VP, Gov't Affairs (RJ Reynolds)	Staff: Rep Boehner (R)
John Hoel	VP, Gov't Affairs (Altria Group)	Staff: Rep Gordon (D)
Paul Carothers	VP, Gov't Affairs (Philip Morris)	Staff: Sen Breaux (D)
David Hayes	Lobbyist (General Cigar Holdings)	Dep Sec of the Interior (Obama)

ENDNOTES

CHAPTER 1

1. As told by Tony Campolo, https://youtu.be/BXnY9YWF-Gg

CHAPTER 2

1. Brennan Manning, *Ruthless Trust*, Harper Collins, 2002, pg. 88
2. For more on this, see *The Reformers and Their Stepchildren* by Leonard Verduin, Christian Hymnary Publishers, 1991
3. As paraphrased by Brian Zahnd in the "Monster God" debate, https://youtu.be/C5M0HBKZlIc
4. Leonard Verduin, *The Reformers and Their Stepchildren*, Christian Hymnary Publishers, 1991
5. John Reisinger, *Tablets of Stone and the History of Redemption,* New Covenant Media, 2004
6. For more information, read *A New Systematic Theology of the Christian Faith* by Dr. Robert L. Reymond

CHAPTER 3

1. Eberhard Arnold, *The Early Christians*, Plough Publishing, pg. 109
2. David Bercot, "What The Early Christians Believed About the Two Kingdoms", https://youtu.be/T2RoCtVueWg
3. Ibid

CHAPTER 4

1. Taken from the book, *The Early Christians*, by Eberhard Arnold, pg. 71-74
2. Ibid.
3. Michael Grant, *Constantine the Great*, pg.140
4. Ibid., page 141
5. Ibid., page 149
6. Justo Gonzalez, *The Story of Christianity*, pg. 107
7. Ibid. page 121
8. Ibid, page 122
9. Ibid, page 124
10. Ibid, page 125
11. For more information, download a free copy of my ebook *This Is My Body:Ekklesia As God Intended* at www.KeithGiles.com
12. From *Tertullians Apology*, chapter 21

CHAPTER 5

1. From his Facebook post, March, 31, 2015
2. Howard Zinn, speaking at Boston University on November 11, 2009, on the subject of American "Holy Wars"
3. William Wilberforce, *A Practical View of Christianity*, pg. 251-252
4. *Parade* Magazine, 1981
5. C.S. Lewis, *The Screwtape Letters*, chapter 7
6. Ed Dobson and Cal Thomas, *Blinded By Might*, pg. 42
7. Ibid, pg. 15
8. Ibid, pg. 96
9. Ibid, pg. 109
10. Ibid, pg.184

11. Ibid, pg. 188

12. Ibid, pg. 189

CHAPTER 6

1. Mary Emily Duba, "Peacemaking and Nonviolence," https://youtu.be/pz0l98v0fnQ

2. G.K. Chesterton, *What's Wrong with the World?*

CHAPTER 7

1. J.W. Coakley, *Readings in World Christian History*, pp. 17-22

2. "How American Evangelicalism Has Been Exploited", April 24, 2015, at www.KeithGiles.com

3. "The Real Origins of the Religious Right" by Randall Ballmer, *Politico*, May, 2014

4. Ibid

5. Ibid

6. Ibid

7. From the PBS Documentary, "God In America", part 6

8. Ibid

9. Ibid

10. Ibid

11. *Blinded By Might*, pg. 23

12. Kevin Kruse, *One Nation Under God: How Corporate America Invented Christian America*

13. Ibid

14. Steve Gregg, *The Narrow Path*, Radio Show, October 3, 2016

15. See http://www.informationclearinghouse.info/article41086.htm

CHAPTER 8

1. This chapter was largely summarized from a presentation given by John Perkins, a former "Economic Hitman" who once participated in this process of exploiting Third World nations and leaders. To learn more, read his book, *Confessions of an Economic Hit Man* and watch the video on YouTube entitled: "John Perkins On Globalization." https://youtu.be/TFC18pFvo1g
2. "Study shows revolving door of employment between Congress and lobbying firms" by T.W. Farnham, *The Washington Post*, September 13, 2011
3. For more on America's foreign interventions, see https://youtu.be/HPExU_VixfQ and https://youtu.be/_WVtpao0KSM
4. For a list of CIA Coups, see https://youtu.be/GZ2grlh9KQI

CHAPTER 9

1. Much of this chapter's information was discovered from the video "Corruption Is Legal In America" https://youtu.be/5tu32CCA_Ig
2. "Pastor Robert Jeffress Explains Support For Trump", *NPR*, October 16, 2016
3. "Is America An Oligarchy?", by John Cassidy, *The New Yorker*, April 18, 2014
4. "When Lobbyists Literally Write The Bill" by Alisa Chang, *NPR*, November 11, 2013.
5. "Corruption Is Legal In America" https://youtu.be/5tu32CCA_Ig
6. Ibid

CHAPTER 10

1. Interview, *Vice News*, June, 2016
2. http://www.asu.edu/feature/includes/spring05/readmore/altheide.html
3. "Despite Grim Media Reports, Crime Rates Are Actually Down In the U.S." by Ari Shapiro, *NPR*, December 23, 2015

4. "If It Bleeds, It Leads", *Psychology Today Magazine*, June 7, 2011
5. https://www.psychologytoday.com/blog/two-takes-depression/201106/if-it-bleeds-it-leads-understanding-fear-based-media
6. http://abcnews.go.com/2020/story?id=2898636&page=1

CHAPTER 11

1. See *Tatian's Address to the Greeks*

CHAPTER 12

1. Leo Tolstoy, *On Patriotism,* 1894

CHAPTER 13

1. Amin Maalouf, *In the Name of Identity: Violence and the Need to Belong,* 2012
2. For a more in-depth examination of Jesus and Non-Violence, download my ebook, *War Is Not Christian,* at Amazon.com
3. From http://www.patheos.com/blogs/formerlyfundie/independence-day-should-christians-celebrate-or-not/

CHAPTER 14

1. Martin Luther King, Jr., "Where Do We Go From Here," an address to the Southern Christian Leadership Conference, August 16, 1967
2. These points adapted from Chuck McKnight's blog post: http://www.beingfilled.com/2014/07/what-did-jesus-think-of-revolution.html
3. Ibid
4. https://www.nationalpriorities.org/campaigns/us-military-spending-vs-world/
5. http://www.upworthy.com/daymn-how-many-years-has-america-been-at-war-since-1776
6. https://en.wikipedia.org/wiki/Chance_for_Peace_speech

7. http://national.deseretnews.com/article/4752/1-in-5-students-are-living-in-poverty.html

8. From his speech at Riverside Church in New York, April 4, 1967

9. https://youtu.be/gU8rQWh_qtc

10. https://youtu.be/iJ5IjSPsC1Y

11. https://youtu.be/md1LM0utRXA

12. https://youtu.be/_PnQdu16RAA

13. http://www.businesspundit.com/the-25-most-vicious-iraq-war-profiteers/

14. http://www.huffingtonpost.com/2008/07/25/iraq-war-profiteers-25-co_n_115004.html

CHAPTER 15

1. Diarmuid Jeffreys, *Hell's Cartel: IG Farben and the Making of Hitler's War Machine,* Holt Paperbacks, 2010

2. Ibid

3. Joseph Borkin, *The Crime and Punishment of I.G. Farben*, Pocket Books, 1979

4. Ibid

5. http://www.mit.edu/~thistle/v13/3/oil.html

6. http://www.washingtonpost.com/wp-srv/national/daily/nov98/nazicars30.htm

7. http://www.lifenews.com/2014/02/23/company-that-made-zyklon-b-for-nazi-holocaust-made-ru-486-for-abortions/

8. Excerpt from *Engaging the Powers*, by Walter Wink

9. Mathew 26:52

10. John 18:36

CHAPTER 16

1. Facebook post: https://www.facebook.com/benjaminlcorey/posts/701550779990830

For more information about Keith Giles
or to contact him for speaking engagements,
please visit *www.KeithGiles.com*

Many voices. One message.

CPSIA information can be obtained
at www.ICGtesting.com
Printed in the USA
BVHW032148250822
645574BV00010B/99